Use Your Tax Dollars to Become a Millionaire

SARAH JONES, CPA, *and* **PHIL D. JONES, JR.**

LUCIDBOOKS

Tax Free Millionaire
Use Your Tax Dollars to Become a Millionaire
Copyright @2026 Sarah Jones, CPA, and Phil D. Jones, Jr.
Published by Lucid Books in Houston, TX
www.LucidBooks.com

ISBN: 978-1-63296-812-8
eISBN: 978-1-63296-813-5

Special Sales: Most Lucid Books titles are available in special quantity discounts. Custom imprinting or excerpting can also be done to fit special needs. Contact Lucid Books at Info@LucidBooks.com

Table of Contents

Introduction   1

Part One

Chapter 1: Debt and the American Dream   7

Chapter 2: Identifying the Need for *Tax Free Millionaire*   11

Chapter 3: You Can't DIY Your Way to Tax Free Wealth   15

Chapter 4: The High Cost of NOT Tax Planning   21

Chapter 5: Hidden Risk of NOT Becoming a
Tax Free Millionaire   25

Chapter 6: The Mind Shift   31

Part Two

Chapter 7: Tax Planning Foundations   55

Chapter 8: The Strategy   61

Chapter 9: The ABC's of Strategies & Loopholes   67

Chapter 10: Meet the Superstar of *Tax Free Millionaire*   107

Chapter 11: Leverage Your Kids   115

Chapter 12: Tale of Two Businesses   119

Chapter 13: The Finish Line   127

Chapter 14: Your Invitation   131

Endnotes   145

About the Authors   147

Introduction

I'm currently writing this in a hotel near the airport in Chicago. Contrary to my Texas roots, I did not show up in boots. I showed up in flip-flops to snowy, windy Chicago. What can I say? Things don't always go as planned, you know? In fact, this entire book was supposed to be something completely different. I had already turned in an almost complete manuscript. So, imagine my publisher's face when I said, "Hold the presses. I've changed my mind!"

If you read my first book, "Fire My CPA" then you know me. I'm Sarah Jones, CPA. I'm a no-nonsense CPA who tells it like it is, always, including in this new book, *Tax Free Millionaire*. Originally, my husband Phil and I set out to write a book about how the American Dream is broken. (You haven't met Phil yet—he's been a financial advisor for over 20 years, a sharp businessman, and an all-around solid human being.)

We wanted to challenge the noise: the analysis paralysis, the overwhelming number of financial options, and the unrealistic expectations people carry around regarding what success should look like. From Dave Ramsey's "Budget-is-Life!" crowd to the "YOLO" mindset that encourages unchecked spending under the belief that tomorrow isn't guaranteed, what to do with money can be a lot to unwrap for the average person who is just trying to live wisely and well.

I still believe the American Dream is broken. I really do. Working 60 years and pinching every penny just to afford a trip to Hawaii? That's not a dream—it's a scam wrapped in red, white, and blue. This book was originally meant to expose the history of debt: how it weighs people down and how the system convinces you that you need a mortgage, maxed-out credit cards, and a mountain of debt just to appear successful.

But then life threw me a curveball, and I had a reckoning.

In the summer of 2024, a huge shift happened in my practice—and it changed the way we did everything. I won't get into all the details, but I will say this: in the middle of the mess, we found something that mattered. And like fertilizer on a lawn, that "mess" forced us to grow.

We shifted.

We started asking bigger questions:

- How do we serve better?
- Lead better?
- Grow stronger?

The answer was clear—*Tax Free Millionaire* needed to shift too. It needed to become a roadmap, a guide for business owners to reclaim their tax dollars, reinvest with purpose, and build lasting generational wealth—without sacrificing today's joy or tomorrow's security.

So what is Tax Free Millionaire, in a nutshell?

It's about taking the tax savings—yes, real money—that we at Sarah Jones, CPA, can find for you at no extra cost. We are setting you up for success by identifying tax dollars you're already leaving on the table. On average, we're talking about saving 20–30% a year, sometimes even more.

But here's the real kicker—it's also about a mindset shift.

We're not just talking about saving you money. We're talking about reinvesting it and leveraging it to build your *Tax Free Millionaire* lifestyle. What does that actually mean? It means building a custom plan that depends on your goals, your business, and your timeline.

That's why Sarah Jones, CPA, will create a personalized *Tax Free Millionaire* roadmap just for you.

Because this isn't one-size-fits-all.

It's about equipping *you*, the business owner, to grow smarter, build wealth intentionally, and keep more of what you earn.

I want you to be a *Tax Free Millionaire* business owner. I want your spouse to become a *Tax Free Millionaire*. And we're going to leverage IRS-compliant strategies to make your kids *Tax Free Millionaire*s too. Just imagine the potential—the power—of taking the money you would've sent to Uncle Sam and investing it back into yourself, your business, and your legacy. That's how you build generational wealth.

And here's the very best part: because we're using tax savings, there's nothing coming out of your pocket. You're not spending, you're simply keeping more of your money and putting it to work to create millions of dollars of tax-free wealth.

As you read this book, you may be thinking I'm just trying to get you to hire me as your CPA. And to be honest, there's some truth in that (because as I said above, I always tell it like it is). But I want to give you real value here, whether you hire me or not, because that's how much I believe in the *Tax Free Millionaire*, and how strongly I believe that you can become one.

Do I have your attention? Let's get started making you a millionaire.

Part One

The *Tax Free Millionaire* System

Chapter 1
Debt and the American Dream

I f you'll recall from my introduction, the original idea behind this book was to talk about how the American Dream is broken—and how we've all been duped into keeping up with the Joneses. Spoiler alert: the Joneses are broke.

Don't get me wrong; I'm incredibly passionate about *Tax Free Millionaire* and everything it stands for. But we can't talk about building tax-free wealth without addressing the foundation of how we've been trained to think about money, success, and what a "dream life" really looks like.

The term "American Dream" came from historian James Truslow Adams in his 1931 book *The Epic of America1*. He described it as "that dream of a land in which life should be better and richer and fuller for everyone, with opportunity for each according to ability or achievement." Notice he didn't mention white picket fences or 30-year mortgages?

The original American Dream was about purpose, about living a life that was meaningful and free, not about collecting things. But somewhere along the line—likely during the rise of industrialization and the modern mortgage industry—that dream shifted. It became about ownership. About having a house (with a big loan), a couple of cars (also financed), a job working for someone else for 40 years, and a vague hope of retiring in your 60s to finally chase the life you wanted all along.

Sound familiar?

In my hometown of Willis, Texas, that's what we were taught: Go to college. Get a job. Work for 40 years. Retire. Then, maybe, enjoy life. I know many of you were fed the same formula.

But here's the thing—it never sat right with me. As a kid, I was a go-getter. People who read *Fire My CPA* know a bit about my story. I had an amazing childhood. I wouldn't change a thing. I had grit, a tight-knit family, and I'm proudly a daddy's girl.

My dad was the hardest-working man I knew, and my mom stayed home with us when we were little. Their values shaped me.

But it was that same environment that sold us a version of the American Dream that revolved around hustle . . . and debt.

The government and financial institutions pushed homeownership hard—and let's be clear, owning a home *is* something to be proud of—but the government and banks also flooded the market with mortgage products that helped people buy homes they couldn't actually afford. And the more stuff people accumulated, the more debt they carried trying to keep up with . . . you guessed it, the Joneses.

As a CPA, I can't disclose names, but I can tell you: I've worked with people who look like they have it all. They drive the right cars, live in the right neighborhoods, go to the right churches—and they're just a couple of paychecks away from financial disaster.

So let me ask you: What's your dream?

I remember thinking I wanted to be a doctor. I said it because it sounded like the "right" goal—the American Dream goal. But once I started anatomy and physiology, I quickly realized: I wasn't cut out for it. (Spoiler: I fainted during a dissection. And I once passed out just from seeing a little blood on my earring after my mom cleaned it. A waterbed and a Kleenex were involved—it was a whole thing.)

The point is: I was chasing a goal that didn't fit *me* because it looked like success from the outside.

So ask yourself: Have you ever sat down and really thought about what you want your life to look like? Your finances? Your family? Your *future*?

Too many of us are living someone else's version of the dream. We're checking boxes we never meant to check. And often, we're doing it in debt.

That's where *Tax Free Millionaire* comes in. This isn't about cutting your spending to the bone or sacrificing your lifestyle. It's about *reclaiming* money you're already handing over to the IRS and redirecting it to fund the life you actually want.

But here's the catch: to stay the course, especially when times get tight, you need a clear *why*.

Your why is what keeps you focused when business is slow, or life gets hard. It's your vision, your motivation, your compass. And yes, working with the right CPA (hi, it's me) can help you improve cash flow and stay on track—but your why is what fuels the journey.

This is not a get-rich-quick plan. This is a *long-term strategy* to build *real, sustainable, tax-free wealth*.

So let me leave you with two questions:

1. If money were no object, what would you do with your life?
2. If money were no object, would you still be doing what you're doing now?

Because that's what we're working toward. That's the dream worth building.

Chapter 2

Identifying the Need for Tax Free Millionaire

I n the Introduction, I asked, "What is a *Tax Free Millionaire?*" That's not a question I can sum up in one short, pithy sentence. On one hand, the concept is too layered for a quick answer—after all, the entire second half of this book is dedicated to walking you through how to become one. But at the same time, the roadmap to get there is actually quite simple. So maybe the best place to start is by explaining what *Tax Free Millionaire* is not.

***Tax Free Millionaire* is not about being tax free,** because that's impossible. The Internal Revenue Service is very clear that paying taxes is not elective. In fact, the federal tax laws and regulations are now over 10 million words long.[2] We have to pay taxes or there are some pretty serious consequences if we don't. We just want to make sure we get you the biggest bang for your tax buck.

Tax Free Millionaire **is not about evading tax.** That's illegal. We're not teaching how to do anything shady, questionable, or illegal. We're kind of sticklers about following the law. We have that in common with the IRS. We aren't coming at you with some under-the-table method of getting you out of paying your taxes. It's not who we are. We're smart, strategic, and most of all sound in our business practices. As a tax-planning CPA, one thing is non-negotiable: we will **never** implement a strategy we can't back up in an audit. Everything we do must be IRS-compliant and fully defensible. Our goal is to give you solid, legitimate strategies that not only save you money, but also give you peace of mind if you're ever audited.

Tax Free Millionaire **is about helping people.** It is helping people just like you to make sure that you are not paying a penny more than you should in tax. We make sure we integrate every single tax strategy that we can for you, then we take all of those savings and leverage them to fund a *Tax Free Millionaire* lifestyle for you, for your spouse, for your kids, and for future generations.

But why do YOU need this? I want you to think about that for a second. It starts by identifying the need.

- Why would you want to become a *Tax Free Millionaire*?
- Why would you want your spouse to become a *Tax Free Millionaire*?
- Why would you want your kids to become *Tax Free Millionaire*s?
- Why do you want to create generational wealth?

Sit with those questions for a minute. Maybe even jot down some reasons if they come to mind.

Becoming a *Tax Free Millionaire* isn't just about having more money—it's about having more freedom, more peace of mind, and more options. I want that for myself so I can live without the constant weight of financial stress, make decisions based on values rather than paychecks, and know I'm maximizing what I've worked so hard to earn. I want my spouse to become a *Tax Free Millionaire* too, because we're building a life together, and true financial freedom is something we should both experience, side-by-side. As for my kids, I want them to grow up with a strong foundation, to learn how to build wealth the right way, and to start their adult lives with choices, not chains. Creating generational wealth is about more than passing on money—it's about passing on wisdom, opportunity, and the ability to live generously and purposefully for generations to come.

Your financial health and well-being are the best ways you can take of yourself and your family. To put it bluntly, money matters. And while money isn't everything, it isn't nothing. Money is not "the root of all evil,"[3] as some might have us think. (And before you come at me, the Bible says, "the **love** of money is the root of all evil.) The truth is that money is neither good nor evil. It is completely neutral.

Money simply reflects what's inside of you. If you're a generous person, you'll be generous with your money. If you're a selfish person, you'll be selfish with your money. If you're a risk-taker in life, you'll be a risk-taker with your money. And if you're cautious in life, you'll be cautious with your money.

Money isn't the problem or the solution. It's a mirror to our mindset.

If you're someone with a scarcity mindset, you may already lean toward being overly cautious—or even a bit selfish—with resources. When you add money to the mix, it amplifies those existing traits. So someone with a scarcity mindset may be overly cautious or selfish with money. They be risk averse and untrusting of other's motives when it comes to their money.

On the flip side, if you are someone with an abundance mindset, you believe there is always an opportunity to make more money. You see money as a tool and enjoy making it so you can give it away. You're operating out of a completely different mindset than the first person we talked about. People who operate from an abundance mindset are likely to be more generous, maybe even more of a risk-taker.

So you have to ask yourself: Why do you want to become a *Tax Free Millionaire*? Sure, you want some tax savings. And of course, you want to stop overpaying in tax. But the bigger reason you should want to become a *Tax Free Millionaire*? It's about what happens **because** you are keeping more of your money. Becoming a *Tax Free Millionaire* means you gain the power to amplify what matters most to you. And we want to help you do that.

Chapter 3

You Can't DIY Your Way to Tax Free Wealth

S arah Jones, CPA, has specialized in tax planning since 2017—and it's the number one reason people are referred to us. Nearly all of our business comes through word-of-mouth. A typical referral sounds like this: "Hey, you saved my brother Jim Bob $20,000 in taxes, and I want those same savings." That's the power of proactive tax strategy—it speaks for itself.

But remember when I said there was a shift in the way we do business? It's because we discovered a very significant disconnect between the value we delivered versus the benefits our clients reaped in tax savings. We realized we had to rethink how we were serving our clients. It wasn't that we lacked clients, far from it. And we were offering real value, designing smart plans, and delivering the tax savings people wanted. But something was off. What I noticed was that I'd set up a plan, the client would be excited, and then I wouldn't hear from them again until tax season.

It seemed like a great plan. We could service hundreds of clients a year that way. We were responsible for doing our part, and they were responsible for doing their part. It was a win-win for the people who did their part. But for the clients who didn't do their part, it wasn't a win. Come year end, I'd review their return and say, "Hey, we talked about integrating X, Y, and Z—but you didn't follow through." And because of that, we couldn't apply the strategies we'd set up for them. They hadn't executed the plan, and we weren't about to file something for them that simply didn't happen.

Sure we'd done our part in setting up the plan, but that was where we saw the disconnect. Our clients needed more from us, and we knew we needed to make a change. That's when we shifted our model. We became one of the first firms I know of to integrate **year-round tax planning.** What that means is: yes, we set you up with a plan—custom-built by Sarah Jones, CPA—but we also walk with you throughout the year. We meet quarterly, adjust as needed, and make sure you're implementing the strategies we've laid out.

Even when life gets crazy, we step in, check in, and push in where needed. "Hey, remember those strategies we put in place? You need to act on them, or you'll lose the benefit." That follow-through is key to the whole plan working. For business owners, when the day-to-day demands are intense, it's easy to let things like tax strategy slide. That's why those quarterly check-ins are so important—they keep your long-term goals on track, even when you're putting out fires.

Step One: Get a tax-planning CPA who works with you year-round

Like any good plan, a solid tax plan is only as good as the people who are executing it. Every day, I meet business owners who've never had a CPA do actual tax planning for them. It's mind-blowing.

Our plan always starts with a **Tax Free Millionaire** Roadmap. Sometimes when I review a potential client's return, I honestly feel like Ashton Kutcher is about to jump out and yell, "You've been punk'd!" (Yes, I'm showing my age with that reference.) Many of these folks have worked with CPAs for years, and their returns are clean and compliant, but there's *no strategy*. They have been overpaying the IRS for years . . . YEARS . . . and that was with a CPA.

Tax Free Millionaire exists to change that. You have to stop overpaying in taxes. Our mission is to take the dollars you're about to hand over to the IRS and redirect them—back into your business, your life, and your legacy.

I believe, and I think you do too, that we are far better stewards of our money than the government is. Regardless of where you fall politically, most of us can agree on that. So let's take those dollars and put them to work building your *Tax Free Millionaire* lifestyle. We're talking about money you were going to pay to the IRS—reclaimed and reinvested into a future of tax-free wealth.

And let me be real with you: I'm not inventing anything new here. These aren't brand-new secrets or some magical tax loophole. I'm not promising something that doesn't exist.

What I am is a CPA who thinks differently. I care deeply about creating massive value and helping people see what's possible when they stop overpaying and start planning. Every CPA in the U.S. follows the same tax code—but not all CPAs choose to practice tax planning. For some, it's just not part of their business model. And others simply don't think outside the box.

That's where Sarah Jones, CPA is different. We're focused on helping our clients get the most from their tax dollars and then to use those tax savings to build long-term, generational wealth. We are driven by helping you create a future where your money is working *for* you—not disappearing into the IRS's hands year after year.

That's what *Tax Free Millionaire* is all about: maximizing your savings and using them to fund a lifestyle of freedom, impact, and legacy.

Step Two: How to know a good CPA from a bad one

Let me start by saying—I'm not here to bash CPAs (or financial advisors). I *am* a CPA. CPAs are the highest level of the accounting world, and I'll say it again: you need to be working with a CPA. Same goes for financial advisors. I've been married to one since 2011. I know firsthand how valuable they can be.

What I *am* here to do is empower you, the reader. That's who I care about serving. I want to help you understand why you need both a CPA and a financial advisor—and why the typical mindset of each might not be enough if your goal is to become a *Tax Free Millionaire*.

The typical CPA is often introverted—nothing wrong with that—but pair that with poor communication skills and a lack of entrepreneurial mindset, and that's where things start to break down. Many CPAs are trained for compliance, not strategy. For example, in my master's program, there wasn't a single course on tax planning. I learned about tax planning from estate planning attorneys—people who went to law school, not accounting school.

Hear me out. Technical accuracy is essential. That's what CPAs are trained to do: keep you compliant and make sure your numbers are right. And that's why you *need* a CPA. You can get into big financial trouble without a CPA. I know of a young entrepreneur who owned a t-shirt business. Call it being at the right place at the right time, but he created a t-shirt with a trending military slogan and was wearing it when a very famous veteran saw him in it. That vet ordered 100,000 t-shirts for the ministry he operated. That young entrepreneur made millions of dollars. And his business partner (who was his friend) told him they didn't need a CPA. All the information they needed about taxes could be found for free online. (And he's not wrong). However, finding information and knowing how to use that information is not always the same thing. And that young entrepreneur ended up owing the IRS hundreds of thousands of dollars because he didn't have a CPA. In short, you need a CPA. Period.

But you also need a CPA who also does *tax planning*. You need someone who's not just accurate, but who thinks like you do. You need someone entrepreneurial—someone who hustles like you do—so you can create solutions together. Without that synergy, it doesn't matter how technically skilled your CPA is. If your CPA is working a booth in a discount store chain, they probably aren't aligned with your energy. If our young entrepreneur had hired a CPA, he might not have owed so much in tax penalties. But if he'd hired the right CPA, he'd likely have saved hundreds of thousands of dollars in overpaid taxes.

Step Three: You Need a Financial Planner Who Talks Truth to You

Not only do you need the right CPA, but you also need the right financial planner. The number one thing any good financial advisor should ask is: "What are your goals?" If you sit down with one, and they immediately start recommending mutual funds or portfolios before understanding your vision, that's a red flag. They're likely more interested in their commission than your future.

A good financial planner is not only going to help you decide how to invest your money, but they are also going to tell you the cold, hard truth when you need it. They'll keep you headed toward good decisions and away from bad ones that will derail your goals.

And if you ever want to build real wealth—or become that elusive *Tax Free Millionaire*—you need to stop chasing income and start building assets, and you need an incredible financial advisor to do that.

I want you to have the right team in place. I want you to have a badass CPA and a badass financial advisor who work *together* to create a winning strategy for *you*. This is what our firm is built on: empowering, inspiring, and creating massive value for our clients. That's the entire mission behind Sarah Jones, CPA. It should be the mission of anyone you trust with your money.

Chapter 4
The High Cost of NOT Tax Planning

W e're getting into the good stuff now: the real price you pay when you don't do tax planning.

As a CPA who specializes in tax planning, I see the impact of inaction every single week. We start with the *Tax Free Millionaire* Roadmap, and when I review a client's previous return, I run the numbers to show how much they could've saved if they had implemented just a few key strategies.

It's almost always the same story: the client sees the savings and immediately feels frustrated with their current CPA. They'll say, "I knew they weren't doing a good job." But I always respond, "Hold on—your return is clean, accurate, and compliant. Did you ever *ask* them to do tax planning?"

Nine times out of ten, the answer is no.

Here's the hard truth: most CPAs don't do tax planning. They do tax preparation. They record what already happened.

But tax planning? That's proactive. It's forward thinking, and it's rare. And I'll say that more than once—because I want it to stick. Don't trust someone online calling themselves a "tax strategist." Anyone can throw around the title "tax strategist." But, if they're not a **CPA** or **JD** (tax attorney), think twice before you hire them. Even Enrolled Agents (I am one, too) may not have the full scope of training to build and defend a comprehensive strategy. You need a credentialed expert—someone who knows the rules *and* how to use them to your advantage.

If you're not actively doing tax planning, you could be losing **millions** over your lifetime. Let's break that down.

Why Most CPAs Don't Plan—and Why You Can't Afford That

Most CPAs are not lazy or bad at their job. They are overworked, buried in deadlines, and trained to avoid risk—not look for opportunity. Many firms are set up like assembly lines: input your data, crank out the return, move to the next client. That works fine for compliance, but it *leaves money on the table*.

And here's where it gets dangerous: people assume their CPA is taking care of their tax strategy just because they're paying them to do their taxes. But unless you've specifically hired someone for *tax planning*, you're probably just getting tax prep.

Let's break this down with an example.

How Much Is "No Plan" Costing You?

Imagine you're 30 years old and you own a business. You're earning a few hundred thousand dollars a year. You decide not to invest in a tax planning CPA because you figure, "I just need to pay my taxes and be done with it." That mindset could cost you big time.

Let's say you're still paying self-employment tax and earning a few hundred thousand dollars a year, you could be overpaying by **tens of thousands**. Now add in the fact that you're not using entity structuring, not leveraging advanced strategies, and not reviewing your numbers quarterly. If your net income is around $400,000, you could easily be overpaying by $100,000 every single year in unnecessary taxes.

Now let that number settle in. **$100,000 a year. $100,000 a year.**

That's money going straight to the IRS that could have been used to grow your business, support your family, or—what this book is all about—build your *Tax Free Millionaire* lifestyle.

And that's just the beginning. If you remember the concept of compound interest, you'll understand this isn't just about one year's overpayment. It's about the opportunity cost of every dollar lost, compounded over time. That's where the real damage comes in. We're talking **millions of dollars lost** over your lifetime— lost to the IRS, without accountability, oversight, or strategy.

Yes, we're all required to pay taxes. But you shouldn't be overpaying. You're a better steward of your money than the IRS, and it's time to start acting like it. You need to take control of your finances and partner with a CPA and financial advisor who will help you keep more of what you earn—and put it to work building real wealth. *Tax Free Millionaire* wealth.

Here's the cold hard truth.

- Your CPA isn't losing sleep if you're overpaying.
- The IRS isn't complaining either.
- Only **you** and your family bear the burden of over-paying tax.

That's the high cost of not tax planning, and it lands squarely on your shoulders. And because it's squarely on your shoulders, you need to know who you're hiring. Don't just hire a "tax strategist." Almost anyone can set up a website, register for a PTIN, and start doing returns under the label of "tax strategist." But not everyone is qualified to guide your financial future. I'll say it again; you need a **CPA** or **tax attorney** guiding your tax strategy, not someone who disappears when the IRS comes calling.

Failing to plan for taxes is expensive.

Choosing the wrong team is too.

Chapter 5
Hidden Risk of NOT Becoming a *Tax Free Millionaire*

Ẃe've talked about what *Tax Free Millionaire* is and how powerful the concept can be. I want that for you. But let's flip the question: **what's the risk of not following the *Tax Free Millionaire Roadmap?*** Well—quite simply, it means you won't become a *Tax Free Millionaire*. And honestly, who doesn't want that? Take a moment and really ask yourself: is there *any* good reason not to pursue it?

Think about it: the system, the solutions, and the roadmap already exist. It's straightforward—and in most cases, it's funded through tax savings, not out-of-pocket costs. So why wouldn't you take advantage of that?

Let's talk about two business owners to illustrate the point: Tom and Kathy.

Tom starts working with Sarah Jones, CPA, in his 30s. He's coachable. He gets a custom-built roadmap, goes through the

Tax Free Millionaire course, works with our team one-on-one, and implements a tax strategy. As a result, let's say he saves $100,000 per year in taxes.

Now, instead of that money going to the IRS, Tom reinvests it. He works with his CPA and financial advisor team—like the one we provide—to direct those funds into tax-free or tax-advantaged investments. That $100,000 per year becomes the fuel for his *Tax Free Millionaire* lifestyle. He made that investment, went through the process, and now he has a custom-built roadmap — a *Tax Free Millionaire* Roadmap guiding his journey to success. We are taking the dollars he saved through strategic tax planning and putting them to work in tax-free investments that are creating a *Tax Free Millionaire* lifestyle for Tom, his wife, his kids, and even his grandkids.

This is what we mean when we say generational wealth.

Now let's talk about Kathy. Kathy also sat down with Sarah Jones, CPA, but she didn't think it was worth the investment to do tax-planning. She convinced herself that she didn't need the benefits being offered. In fact, she wasn't too sure ole' Sarah Jones wasn't just out to make a quick buck off of her. So Kathy stayed with her current CPA. Unfortunately, his methods are as outdated as the 1985 Camry he drives. But you know, he's compliant, and he produces a mean tax return for Kathy every year.

Kathy's CPA is good, he's reliable, but he's not strategic. He's never brought her new ideas, no tax-planning information, and in fact, he still has Kathy paying self-employment tax. Kathy's not taking advantage of any strategies, any loopholes. She's not optimizing her entity setup, and she owns multiple businesses that she has had for quite some time.

TAX FREE *Millionaire*

Sarah Jones CPA

| END AMOUNT | ADDITIONAL CONTRIBUTION | RETURN RATE | STARTING AMOUNT | INVESTMENT LENGTH |

Starting Amount	0
After	20 YEARS
Return Rate	12
Compound	ANNUALLY
Additional Contribution	100,000

Contribute at the ☐ beginning ☐ end

of each ☐ month ☐ year

Calculate

Results

End Balance	$7,205,244.24
Starting Amount	$0.00
Total Contributions	$2,000,000.00
Total Interest	$5,205,244.24

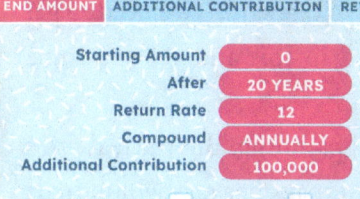

INVESTMENT CALCULATOR

Accumulation Schedule
ANNUAL SCHEDULE   MONTHLY SCHEDULE

YEAR	DEPOSIT	INTEREST	ENDING BALANCE
1	$100,000.00	$0.00	$100,000.00
2	$100,000.00	$12,000.00	$212,000.00
3	$100,000.00	$25,440.00	$337,440.00
4	$100,000.00	$40,492.80	$477,932.80
5	$100,000.00	$57,351.94	$635,284.74
6	$100,000.00	$76,234.17	$811,518.90
7	$100,000.00	$97,382.27	$1,008,901.17
8	$100,000.00	$121,068.14	$1,229,969.31
9	$100,000.00	$147,596.32	$1,477,565.63
10	$100,000.00	$177,307.88	$1,754,876.51
11	$100,000.00	$210,584.82	$2,065,458.33
12	$100,000.00	$247,855.00	$2,413,313.33
13	$100,000.00	$289,597.60	$2,802,910.93
14	$100,000.00	$336,349.31	$3,239,260.24
15	$100,000.00	$388,711.23	$3,727,971.47
16	$100,000.00	$447,356.58	$4,275,328.04
17	$100,000.00	$513,039.37	$4,888,367.41
18	$100,000.00	$586,604.09	$5,574,971.50
19	$100,000.00	$668,996.58	$6,343,968.08
20	$100,000.00	$761,276.17	$7,205,244.24

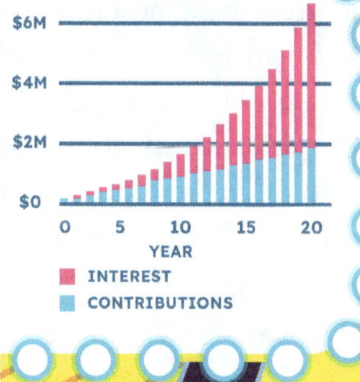

■ INTEREST
■ CONTRIBUTIONS

ANDREW LAITINEN

And to top it off, Kathy's CPA has never even mentioned the real estate loopholes she could be using. She owns multiple properties, but they're all sitting in one LLC — not ideal for asset protection. No one flagged it. No one said, "We need to get an estate planning attorney involved in this and get you some asset and liability protection."

So Kathy chose not to pay for tax planning. But the real price tag on that decision is that Kathy overpays her tax by hundreds of thousands of dollars in her lifetime, and these dollars go to the IRS. If Kathy had hired Sarah Jones, CPA and gotten a *Tax Free Millionaire* Roadmap in her thirties, everything could have been different. All of those hundreds of thousands of dollars that went to the IRS? They could have been redirected back into her pocket. With the right mindset shift, a solid plan, and a clear strategy, she could have used those funds to build real wealth for her, her husband, and her kids. She could have built a *Tax Free Millionaire* lifestyle.

Now here's the key point: the risk of not doing this—of not building your own *Tax Free Millionaire* plan—is the millions of dollars you're giving up in tax-free wealth. And it's not from extra income. It's from the tax savings you already *could* have had.

Most business owners are overpaying in taxes—by 20 to 30% or more each year—simply because they're not working with a CPA who specializes in tax planning. And here's the real cost: it's not just this year's overpayment. It's the missed opportunity to build wealth, impact your family, and change your financial legacy.

If you implement tax planning and reinvest those savings wisely, you can create life-changing results—for yourself, your spouse, your children, even your grandchildren. You can literally rewrite your family tree.

That's what this is about. And in the next few chapters, we're going to shift your mindset and get you ready to take action. These chapters are short but powerful. They're designed to get you thinking deeply—about your goals, your future, and your financial potential.

Tax Free Millionaire isn't about theory. It's about transformation. And it starts by leveraging dollars you're already spending—tax dollars that would otherwise go to the IRS—and redirecting them into smart, strategic investments. That's why I'm inviting you to take the next step.

Scan the QR code below or visit www.TaxFreeMillionaireSystems.com—we've packed it with valuable, affordable resources to help you get started.

Let's keep moving—onto the next chapter. Your roadmap begins now.

Chapter 6

The Mind Shift

I f I had to pick one chapter that could change everything, it's this one.

Why? Because before you become a *Tax Free Millionaire*, you have to *think* like one. And that starts with a serious mind shift.

What happens if you *don't* invest in tax-planning, in a solid tax strategy?

You could end up overpaying hundreds of thousands—maybe even millions—in taxes over your lifetime. Yes, millions. Heck, like Kathy, it could cost you nearly 10 million dollars over a lifetime. That depends on your age, your business size, and the kind of strategic planning you're doing—or not doing. This isn't theoretical. It's real money. Your money. And the stakes are high: your goals, your freedom, your future.

But what if you *did* have a roadmap? What if you worked with a CPA who doesn't just do taxes once a year, but offers *year-round* planning? Who helps you reduce your tax burden *and* shows you how to invest those saved dollars wisely?

Let me be clear: I'm not reinventing the wheel here. I'm doing strategic tax planning in a way that actually makes sense and funds a powerful, tax-free lifestyle. This isn't magic. It's strategy. And it works.

At Sarah Jones CPA, our mission is simple: **Build. Protect. Grow.** We help you build your dreams, protect your assets, and grow your legacy. That's what we're here to do, and it all starts with a roadmap—your very own *custom-built* plan.

The Game of Life, CPA Edition

Remember the game *Life*? I used to play it at my grandmommy's house as a kid. You start in a little plastic car, maybe pick up a spouse and some kids along the way, and travel through different lands. That game was fun—but real life is no board game.

Still, the concept inspired our custom roadmap at Sarah Jones CPA. We walk with you through the "lands" of life and business, making sure you're getting the most value at every turn.

Let me break down the three parts of our roadmap:

1. Build – Build Your Dreams

This is where it starts. And to be honest? It's not the sexy stuff. This is the work that most people want to skip. But without it, nothing else works.

Most readers of this book are business owners—or they want to be. So "Build" means laying the *right* foundations: bookkeeping, accounting systems, processes, and leveraging AI in a strategic way. Think QuickBooks Online, reconciled reports, CPA oversight, and a CFO dashboard (yep, we provide one to all our clients), that helps you drive real time strategies in your business.

You cannot skip this part. If your business is built on shaky ground, the first storm that comes along will knock it down. So before we talk about tax strategy or growing wealth, we build stability. We figure out what your end goals are and reverse-engineer your plan from there.

2. Protect – Protect Your Assets

Now that you've built something worth protecting, let's make sure nothing takes it away.

This is the land of tax strategy, tax compliance, and risk management. It's where we do year-round planning to reduce your tax bill, shield your assets, and legally structure your business to hedge risk. We put the right team around you to make sure you—and your family—are secure.

All that hard work in "Build" means nothing if you leave yourself exposed. Our job is to make sure that doesn't happen.

3. Grow – Grow Your Legacy

Here's the fun part. This is where your hard work starts to pay off.

Once we've built and protected, we move into growth—real, strategic growth. This is where the *Tax Free Millionaire* Strategy shines. We take those tax savings from "Protect" and leverage them into tax-free investments that accelerate your results.

This is where you begin to grow your legacy—and become a *Tax Free Millionaire*. Take a second. Say that out loud:

"I am going to be a *Tax Free Millionaire*."

Feels good, doesn't it?

Especially if you didn't grow up believing that was possible. If you were raised with a scarcity mindset or told that wealth wasn't for people like you—it can be hard to believe. But let me be the one to tell you, it *is* possible. And it starts right now.

It's Not Too Late

You might be reading this and thinking, "But I'm 40," or "I've made so many mistakes," or "I'm starting too late." Listen, I'm 43 and writing this book from a hotel room in Chicago. If I can do this, so can you. If I can start a revolution and transform an industry way overdue for a transformation, then you can start succeeding today.

It is true, time is one of the most powerful contributors to building wealth. The earlier you start, the better—but it's never too late to begin.

What's important now is your *mindset*. Prime your mind. Open your heart. You need to *believe* this is possible before you can start building it. That's why this chapter matters so much. Because without the right mindset, all the strategies in the world won't stick.

Your Roadmap Starts Here

Tom decided to get proactive. He worked with us, saved millions in taxes over the course of his career, and invested that money in tax-advantaged vehicles. By the time he exited his business, he was a tax-free multimillionaire.

Kathy, on the other hand, didn't want to spend the time or money on planning. She overpaid in taxes year after year. When she finally sold her business, she didn't have an exit strategy in place and lost even more to taxes. Despite being a successful business owner, she left millions on the table.

She couldn't fully fund a 401(k), couldn't take advantage of tax-efficient accounts, and ended up exiting her business with no real retirement plan. Like many owners, she assumed her business *was* her retirement. But without a strategy, she paid far more to the IRS than she needed to—and didn't have enough left to fund the future she deserved.

So here's the big question: do you want to be like Tom or like Kathy?

Picture yourself at the end of your career. You've built something great. Do you want to look back knowing you paid more in taxes than necessary? Or do you want to know you captured those dollars, reinvested them, and created lasting wealth for your family?

The opportunity is right in front of you. A lifetime of potential, funded by money you're already spending—only this time, not to the IRS.

You decide.

You need a custom roadmap. You need the *right* team. You need a CPA who knows how to think bigger. That's what we do at Sarah Jones CPA. We take the tax dollars you're already wasting and turn them into fuel for your future wealth.

You need a *badass* CPA and a *badass* financial advisor.

If you love your current CPA or advisor? Great—share this book with them. You can take advantage of our resources and have them implement them for you. But if they're not willing to adopt this level of strategy, then I'm sorry . . . they're not the ones for you.

And if you're still feeling hesitant—if you've had failures, or things haven't worked out before—let me tell you again:

this is not complicated. It's not magic. It's strategy. It's not new money—it's the money you're already giving to the IRS, redirected to build your future.

And it starts right here—with you believing it's possible. Because the second half of this book is where we are going to be giving you the strategies you need to turn your belief into a reality.

Head to **TaxFreeMillionaireSystem.com** (or scan the QR code at the bottom of this page) and access resources—including a full course, a *Tax Free Millionaire* Roadmap, and more. Even if you're not ready to work with us one-on-one, there's something there to help you start now.

Before we jump into Part Two, The *Tax Free Millionaire* Roadmap, I wanted to share with you exactly what we bring to the tax strategy table. It gives you a high level overview of what we offer, as well as the full scope of SJCPA.

WELCOME to *Sarah Jones* CPA

VIP   VIP

Land of Grow:
GROW Your Legacy
Wealth Management
Insurance Protection
Exit and Succession Planning
Coaching and Courses
VIP with Sarah

PITSTOP
Annual SJCPA Conference
Fire My CPA
Tax Free Millionaire
Weekly Tips

PITSTOP
Free Tax Roadmaps
SJCPA Academy
Open House
Weekly Q&A with Sarah

Land of Protect:
PROTECT Your Assets
Tax Compliance
Year Round Tax Planning
Estate Planning

FOOD!

JUST MARRIED

$$$

Land of Build:
BUILD Your Dreams
Bookkeeping
CFO Services
Advisory Services

Start Position:
ONBOARDING

ILLUSTRATED BY ANDREW LATTINEN

38

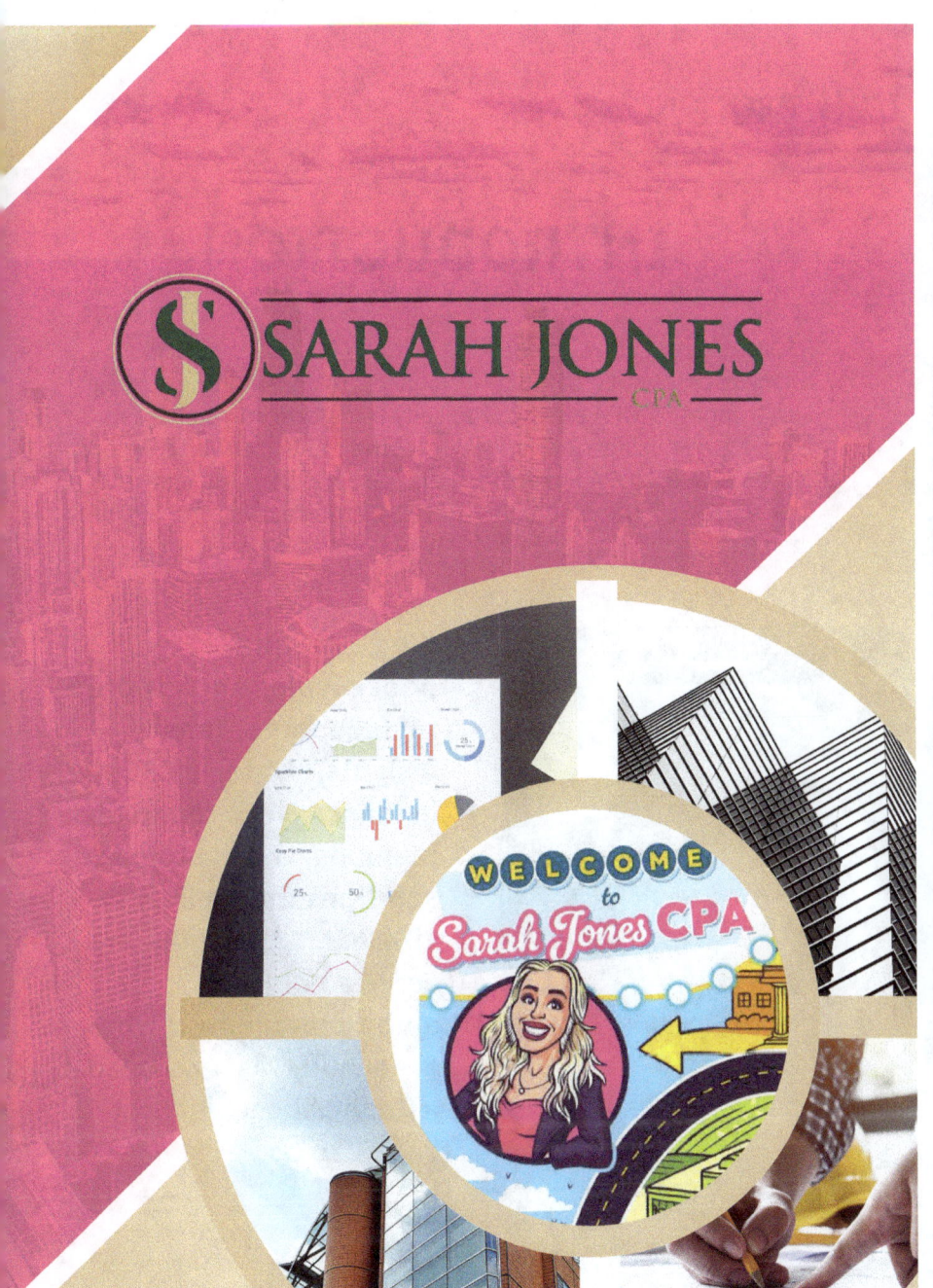

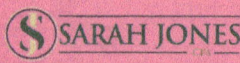

INTRODUCTION

SJCPA is not your traditional CPA firm, we are your strategic financial partner. Founded by visionary CPA and financial strategist Sarah Jones, SJCPA exists to radically transform how seven and eight-figure business owners navigate their financial world. Through our exclusive SJCPA Roadmap, we guide elite entrepreneurs on a journey to BUILD their dreams, PROTECT their assets, and GROW their legacy.

We go beyond bookkeeping and tax prep to deliver real-time insights, strategic CFO guidance, year-round tax planning, and customized solutions that deliver a 10X ROI. We proudly serve a bold and ambitious clientele who are scaling fast and need a financial partner that can keep up.

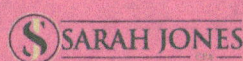

BUILD
BUILD YOUR DREAMS

At SJCPA, everything begins with BUILD, the foundational pillar of our Roadmap. We don't just balance your books, we help you build a powerful financial structure that supports sustainable growth, profitability, and clarity.

For seven and eight-figure business owners, traditional bookkeeping simply isn't enough. You need strategic insight, expert-level financial leadership, and a team that sees the big picture. That's where we come in.

Through outsourced CFO services, customized budgeting, team accountability design, and business advisory, we deliver the tools and guidance you need to drive results.

With decades of financial analysis experience and our proprietary Roadmap Design, SJCPA delivers clarity, confidence, and measurable ROI at every step of your business journey.

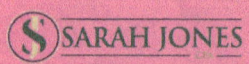

BUILD SERVICES

Outsourced CFO Services

Get high-level financial strategy without the full-time cost. We guide your business with the expertise of a seasoned CFO to drive clarity, performance, and growth.

Accounting and Advisory

More than just numbers — we interpret your financials, advise on business decisions, and ensure your accounting is always aligned with your strategic goals.

Budget & Roadmap Design

Custom financial roadmaps and dynamic budgets to help you track goals, measure progress, and stay in control.

Cash Flow Design and Analysis

We map, monitor, and optimize your cash flow to ensure your business is healthy, agile, and prepared for opportunity.

Team Accountability & KPI Design

We help build out systems and scorecards to drive performance and accountability across your team.

Business Coaching and Design

With a mix of financial insight and entrepreneurial coaching, we help refine your business model, improve operations, and unlock long-term value.

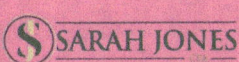

PROTECT
PROTECT YOUR ASSETS

After building a strong financial foundation, the next step in the SJCPA Roadmap is PROTECT — because what you've built deserves to be shielded with intention, strategy, and long-term vision.

At SJCPA, protection isn't passive — it's proactive. We specialize in year-round tax planning, estate structuring, and compliance strategies that don't just save you money — they unlock it.

While most firms only show up at tax time, we walk with our clients all year long. We develop and implement custom-built tax strategies that consistently save our clients millions over their business life cycle — helping them move toward tax-free millionaire status.

We protect not just your bottom line, but your legacy, your family, and your future.

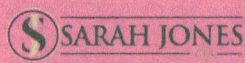
PROTECT SERVICES

Tax Compliance

Ensure your business is always up to date and compliant with federal, state, and local tax regulations — accurately, efficiently, and on time.

Tax Plan Design

Custom-built tax strategies crafted specifically for your business structure, industry, and financial goals — designed to optimize savings.

Year-Round Tax Planning

We don't just check in during tax season. Our team provides ongoing, proactive tax planning throughout the year to maximize deductions and minimize liabilities.

Estate Planning

Protect your wealth and pass it on with intention. Our estate planning strategies help safeguard your assets, reduce estate taxes, and preserve your legacy.

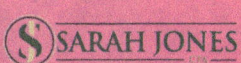
GROW
GROW YOUR LEGACY

Once your business is built and protected, it's time to GROW — your wealth, your impact, and your legacy.

This is where strategy meets purpose. At SJCPA, we help successful entrepreneurs like you scale beyond numbers into true legacy creation. Whether you're preparing for a strategic exit, building generational wealth, or launching your next big vision — we're here to elevate every step.

Our exclusive VIP programs, wealth management services, and tailored succession planning aren't just about adding value — they're about multiplying it. With SJCPA, growth isn't random. It's strategic, intentional, and deeply aligned with your why.

Through one-on-one coaching, advanced planning, and curated solutions, we guide elite business owners toward their fullest potential — in business and in life.

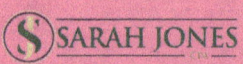
SARAH JONES

GROW SERVICES

Wealth Management

Customized, strategic planning to grow and preserve your wealth — aligned with your long-term goals, values, and legacy vision.

Strategic Insurance Solutions

Use insurance as a powerful financial tool to protect, plan, and grow. From risk mitigation to wealth transfer, we align your coverage with your bigger picture.

Exit and Succession Planning

Whether you're selling, merging, or passing on your business, we design smart exit strategies that maximize value and ensure a seamless transition.

Coaching and Courses

Exclusive access to powerful business education, frameworks, and mentorship to fuel continuous growth and leadership.

VIP with Sarah

Our most elite, results-driven program. Work one-on-one with Sarah Jones, CPA to gain 10x ROI through personalized strategy, coaching, and accountability

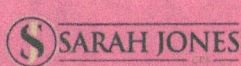
SARAH JONES

SJCPA PITSTOPS
POWERFUL TOOLS. MEANINGFUL CONNECTIONS. ZERO COST.

Every great journey includes meaningful stops along the way— moments to refuel, reflect, and re-energize. At SJCPA, we've built Pitstops into our Roadmap to deliver high-value, FREE tools, education, and experiences that empower seven and eight-figure business owners all year long.

Just like a Buc-ee's stop on a Texas road trip, our Pitstops are packed with value — minus the price tag. Whether it's a hands-on workshop, a virtual session with our expert team, or access to cutting-edge financial strategies, we make sure you're never traveling alone.

These Pitstops are designed to keep you informed, inspired, and in control of your business journey. Because at SJCPA, your success isn't seasonal — it's year-round.

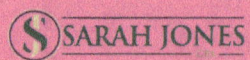
SARAH JONES

PITSTOPS SERVICES

Tax Free Millionaire – Book & Course

Learn the exact strategies used by top entrepreneurs to create tax-efficient wealth and long-term success.

Tax Free Millionaire Conferences

Deep dives into wealth-building and tax-saving strategies that can transform your financial future.

Fire My CPA – Book & Course

A no-nonsense guide to breaking free from traditional, outdated CPA models and stepping into smart financial leadership.

Weekly Tax Tips

Actionable advice delivered straight to your inbox — because real savings happen year-round, not just at tax time.

Annual SJCPA Conference

Held every January in Houston — a must-attend event packed with insights, networking, and expert-led strategy sessions.

SJCPA Academy

A learning platform filled with resources, masterclasses, and insider content to sharpen your financial skill set.

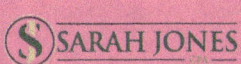
PITSTOPS SERVICES

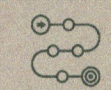

Free Annual Roadmap Design

Every client receives a customized roadmap to align vision, growth, and profitability — updated annually to stay on course.

Open House Events

Meet the SJCPA team, connect with peers, and gain exclusive behind-the-scenes insights into our process.

Weekly Q&A Sessions

Live access to our expert team — bring your questions, get clarity, and move forward with confidence.

SARAH JONES

WHY CHOOSE US?

Because you deserve more than just tax preparation. You deserve a strategic partner. At Sarah Jones, CPA, we go beyond the basics to deliver year-round, done-for-you tax planning that builds wealth, protects your legacy, and keeps you fully IRS-compliant.

01

OVER 15 YEARS OF EXPERIENCE

Sarah brings deep expertise in guiding business owners through complex financial decisions, tax laws, and wealth-building strategies.

02

TAX STRATEGY LEADER

Known for her innovative and proactive approach, Sarah has helped redefine how high-income entrepreneurs approach tax planning.

03

HIGH-GROWTH PROFILES

Her focus is on seven- and eight-figure earners who need advanced, customized strategies not cookie-cutter solutions.

04

PROVEN TRACK RECORD OF ROI

Clients consistently achieve significant tax savings year over year often in the range of 20–30% thanks to Sarah's precision planning.

05

100% IRS-COMPLIANT STRATEGIES

Every tactic used in the Tax-Free Millionaire System is fully vetted for compliance, ensuring peace of mind and audit protection.

06

STRATEGIC, NOT REACTIVE PLANNING

Unlike traditional CPA's Sarah doesn't just file returns she builds long-term financial blueprints that drive growth and protect legacies.

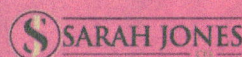

SARAH JONES

FOUNDER MESSAGE

I am so thankful you are here! Most likely, you are a seven or eight-figure business owner who has been looking for a CPA who gets you. Someone who is like-minded. Most CPA's are ill-equipped to keep up with your pace. Most can't get on board with your vision and most can't provide CFO and tax planning services that are 10X ROI. But, I wanted to create a CPA firm unlike anything ever seen. Something that was a game-changer. An industry over-turner. And why? Because our industry is WAY OVERDUE for a change. Most CPA's can't communicate, they give low-level service, offer outdated advice, and do NOT serve you or your business. Quit messing around with "bookkeeping" services and once-a-year tax services.

Enter SJCPA. I created my firm because I am passionate about change. I am passionate about YOU. Your goals, your dreams and your success. When you win, we win together.

Take a look around. Visit our website. Grab a copy of our books. Book a strategy session with our team. Come to one of our conferences, or jump on one of our QA sessions. Connect with us on social media.

If you are that seven or eight-figure business owner who wants to 10X their results, 10X their tax savings, and 10X their business momentum, reach out to me personally to see if the VIP program with Sarah may be just what you are looking for.

And never settle. Your dreams, your WHY, your family and your life....deserve nothing but the best.

BUILD, PROTECT, GROW,

Sarah Jones, CPA

Part Two

The *Tax Free Millionaire* System

Chapter 7

Tax Planning Foundations

Welcome to the *Strategies*. Welcome to the *meat and potatoes* **of** *Tax Free Millionaire*. For those of you who jumped straight to this section—hi, glad you're here. I've read half a million business books, flipping through them to get to the "good stuff." But let me offer this: Chapters 1 through 6 are where the mindset work happens. It lays the groundwork for everything we're about to build. You can't pour a solid foundation if you don't do the groundwork first. So if you need to, take the time to circle back, do the internal work, and make sure the groundwork is level, solid, and ready to go before moving forward.

Tax Planning Foundations

I'm a CPA, an EA, and a Certified Tax Planner. This is my jam. I told you in the Introduction that I know at times it will seem like the point of this book is to get you to hire Sarah Jones, CPA. But I want you to succeed and be a *Tax Free Millionaire*—

period. I also promised to give you actionable information that you can use whether you hire me or not. This information is how we onboard new clients. It's important because it gives you an idea of what your CPA should be doing with you.

Let me walk you through how the process typically starts at least at *Sarah Jones, CPA*. It all begins with your *Tax Free Millionaire* Roadmap. We give you access to a secure portal where you upload your tax documents. Once we've reviewed everything, we present you with your custom **Tax Free Millionaire Roadmap** that tells you:

- Exactly how much we can save you in taxes
- How those tax savings could be used to fund your *Tax Free Millionaire* lifestyle
- And what your tax-free wealth could look like 10, 20, 30 years down the road

But before we can *fund* that dream, we have to *find* the money. That's where the foundations come in.

Before we dive into the building blocks of the foundations, we have to start with clarity. Knowing where you stand financially is the first step to figuring out where you can go. That's why we begin with a simple but powerful *Tax Free Millionaire* Roadmap, so you can see exactly where the money is hiding and how to put it to work.

- **It Starts with Your Books**

  Is your bookkeeping accurate? Is it clean? Because if your books are a mess, your taxes will be too. It's that simple. Garbage in, garbage out. Your financials are the foundation for every tax-saving strategy we'll talk about, and if that data is off, so is your entire plan. If your books are a mess, you're likely overpaying in taxes. Messy books lead to missed deductions, misreported income, and ultimately, overpaying the IRS. That's low-hanging fruit. Cleaning up your books is one of the easiest ways to uncover hidden savings and take control of your financial future. Bonus: having accurate data helps you make decisions in your business, gain clarity, and drive strategy.

- **The Self-Employment Tax Trap**
  Because many of our clients are business owners, we consider this topic foundational. It all starts with Line 23 on the form 1040. Are you paying self-employment tax? Sometimes that's unavoidable, but not always. How you're structured as a business makes all the difference and can lead to significant savings. If you're a sole proprietor, single-member LLC, or a general partner, chances are you're paying **self-employment tax**—also known as what I call the *stupid tax*. It's not that I think *you're* stupid. (You wouldn't be reading this book if that were true.) It's just that I think it's stupid to overpay tax when you don't have to.

Here's how it works:
- When you were a W-2 employee, you paid 7.65% in Social Security and Medicare taxes. Your employer paid the other 7.65%.
- But when you're self-employed, you're on the hook for the *whole* 15.3%.

That's $15,000 on every $100,000 of profit—money that could be working for you. With the *right entity structure*, you may be able to legally reduce or eliminate that. And that's certainly something we will help you with; but how you structure your business depends upon your goals. Your goals are central to *everything* we do.

- **Set Financial Goals That are Specific to You**
  You absolutely have to have financial goals, and you absolutely have to have a CPA who keeps those goals in mind when it comes to tax-planning and your overall financial strategy

  Let me give you a real-world example. One of my long-time clients from New Jersey referred me to a friend of his. The original client was focused on long-term wealth, so we implemented advanced tax and estate planning strategies to help him build generational wealth. His friend, on the other hand, was heavily involved in commercial real estate. For him, showing *income* on paper was critical to maintaining bankability for loans and cash flow.

  The same tax-saving strategies that helped the first client wouldn't work for the second one and could've even hurt him financially. This is why you need a *custom plan*. Tax strategy must be tailored to your goals, your industry, and your future.

- **Think Like an Owner: Plan for the Exit**
  Let me plant this seed now: if you're not thinking about your **exit strategy**, why are you even in business? You've

poured your blood, sweat, and tears into your company. One day, you'll sell it. And when that time comes, you'll *want* to sell it the right way. Too often, business owners don't think about this until the sale is already happening. I've heard so many say, "Well, I guess I'll just pay the tax." But there's so much more you can do. Exit planning is one of the most powerful tools you can leverage, and I say that as a **Certified Exit Planning Advisor.** (Yes, that's a real thing.)

If you plan ahead, you can structure your exit to be incredibly tax efficient. With a great exit plan, more of your hard-earned money stays with *you* instead of going to the IRS. This is something we do, and it's something a good CPA should be doing with you.

Your Next Step

The bottom line is this: *you need a CPA who does tax-planning.* Period. You need real eyes on every piece of your financial picture and create a custom *Tax Free Millionaire* Roadmap that outlines:

- How much we can save you
- Which strategies will get you there
- How those savings can fund your future tax-free wealth

This isn't guesswork. This is strategy—tailored to you, created for you by Sarah Jones, CPA. Let's build your foundation right so you can grow something big.

Chapter 8
The Strategy

Y ou've laid the groundwork, poured the foundation, now it's time to learn the strategies to make you a *Tax Free Millionaire*. Now, let's talk strategy. Tax-saving strategies, to be exact.

In the last chapter, we introduced the concept of tax-planning foundations—how it all begins with evaluating your entity setup and completing a comprehensive *Tax Free Millionaire* Roadmap with Sarah Jones, CPA. This chapter is where we dig into what those strategies might look like. But I want to offer a little disclaimer up front: tax-planning isn't static. Strategies change, sometimes year-to-year, sometimes within the same year, depending on new laws, regulations, leadership, and even the political climate.

So if you're reading this in 2025, that's great. But if it's 2028 or beyond, the specifics may have shifted. That's why everything we do at Sarah Jones, CPA is individualized and up-to-date. The strategies in this chapter will give you a high-level view—but for actionable insight, get your *Tax Free Millionaire* Roadmap from us. Updated resources will always be available at www.taxfreemillionairesystem.com.

What Is Tax Strategy?

First, let's define it. A tax strategy is different from a loophole (we'll talk about those later). Strategy is about aligning your tax setup, structure, and decisions with your long-term goals. And yes, that means sometimes it's about changing your entity type—maybe moving from a sole proprietorship to an S Corp or forming a parent or management company.

And as I said earlier, everyone's situation is different. Maybe you're in real estate and need to show more income to remain bankable. Or maybe you're in growth mode and need to minimize self-employment tax. There are just entirely too many possible scenarios to cover it all here, but you can be sure we *do* cover it fully in your Roadmap, as any good CPA should be doing.

Whatever your scenario, we evaluate it all—your structure, cash flow, and future plans. Then we reverse engineer a plan that supports your specific path.

Our Strategy Process

Here's how it works at Sarah Jones, CPA. You start by uploading all your returns—every entity, every personal return—for the most recent year or two. We look at the full picture and trends in your growth, expenses, and structure. We talk through your goals, where your business is headed, and what's most important to you.

From there, we build your custom strategy. Maybe you're a single-member LLC, and we identify that as a red flag. Maybe it's time to restructure. Or maybe you're better off forming a trust or an umbrella entity. We assess and align.

Then we quantify it: what you're currently paying, what you could be saving, and how those tax savings—dollars you're already sending to the IRS—can be redirected to build tax-free wealth.

And guess what? We do all of this at a super affordable rate. We give you roadmaps so you can walk away empowered with clarity, ready to implement with your CPA (or with us of course).

That's right. The custom report, the *Tax Free Millionaire* Roadmap the projections—we do it because we believe in this system. The results are often mind-blowing. We're talking tens—or even hundreds—of thousands of dollars in potential savings. And that's before we even start leveraging those dollars to fund your *Tax Free Millionaire* lifestyle.

From Plan to Execution

One thing I've learned: a great plan means nothing if it's not implemented.

Early in my career, I'd create detailed tax plans, only to circle back months later and find they were never executed. That's why we now offer full-service, year-round tax planning. It's not handholding. It's strategic. We walk with you from beginning to end, ensuring you stay compliant, implement each strategy properly, and actually realize the savings we identified.

At Sarah Jones, CPA, we don't just create the plan—we help you live it out. Every client gets a *Tax Free Millionaire*

Roadmap, a tax plan tailored to your goals, and a team that helps bring it to life.

Even if you and your identical twin walked into my office, you'd each get a unique plan. Because your dreams, your goals, your legacy—they're yours alone. And we honor that.

So let's build your roadmap. Let's turn wasted tax dollars into lasting wealth. And let's make you a *Tax Free Millionaire.*

Your Next Step

To succeed with the *Tax Free Millionaire* System, you need two things:

1. A **CPA** who understands proactive tax planning
2. A **financial advisor** who can help you grow and protect your wealth in a tax-efficient way.

So, if you already have a financial advisor and CPA you trust—amazing. **Your next step** is to have them read this book. Share it with them. We're not here to hoard the knowledge—we're here to elevate the standard. Bottom Line: we want to help as many people as possible live out the *Tax Free Millionaire* lifestyle.

For Everyone Else . . . If you don't have a rockstar CPA or financial advisor—and let's be honest, most people don't—then *we* are your tools. **Your Next Step** is to visit www.taxfreemillionairesystem.com or scan the QR code below to access:

- A **completely free webinar** packed with high-value content
- Affordable resources and downloads to help you understand the system
- A **comprehensive course** (available for purchase) that gives you everything you need to implement the *Tax Free Millionaire* plan with your existing team, if you have one

But hear me on this: **do not try to do this alone**. This isn't a DIY weekend project. Real tax strategy requires the expertise of professionals who do this every day.

Your tools are ready. The roadmap is waiting. Head to www. taxfreemillionairesystem.com or scan the QR code to get your *Tax Free Millionaire* Roadmap—the exact strategy to maximize your savings, protect your assets, and create lasting legacy wealth.

Let's make it happen.

Chapter 9
The ABC's of Strategies & Loopholes

T his chapter is quite literally the ABCs of our *Tax Free Millionaire* Roadmap Design. I've laid them out for you in alphabetical order because every one of these that you qualify for should be a part of your *Tax Free Millionaire* strategy. As surprising as it might sound, many of these are overlooked by CPAs simply because they don't know their clients well enough to know what tax-credits they are eligible to receive. (Of course that's not what happens at Sarah Jones CPA because it's built into your roadmap to fully understand the scope of your financial picture!)

Adoption Assistance

If you're planning to adopt a child, there's good news: for 2025, families may qualify for an adoption tax credit of up to $17,280 per child.

Eligible expenses include:
- Adoption agency fees
- Court costs
- Attorney fees
- Travel expenses directly related to the adoption

Keep in mind, this credit is subject to income phase-out limits — meaning higher-income families may see a reduced benefit. We can walk you through the rules and help you determine exactly how much of the credit you qualify for.

American Opportunity Credit

Great news for college students and their families! For 2025, the American Opportunity Tax Credit (AOTC) can provide up to $2,500 per eligible student.

Eligibility highlights:
- Must be enrolled at least half-time in a degree or certificate program
- Covers qualified expenses like tuition, fees, and course materials
- Available for the first four years of higher education

Income limits do apply, as the credit begins to phase out at higher levels of modified adjusted gross income.

One of the best features is that up to 40% of the credit (up to $1,000) is refundable. That means you could receive part of the credit even if you owe no taxes.

Augusta Rule

The "Augusta Rule" (named after the Augusta Masters golf tournament) is one of the most powerful — and often overlooked — tax strategies for business owners.

How it works:

- You can rent out your personal residence to your business for up to 14 days per year.
- The rent received is tax free to you personally, yet your business can still deduct the expense as long as it's legitimate.

Key requirements:

- A reasonable rental rate study must support the rental value in your area.
- An IRS-compliant rental agreement must be in place.
- Detailed records of meetings and business activities held in your home are required.
- Local regulations must be followed.

This strategy can be especially valuable if you live in a high-demand area where short-term rental rates are high. For example, one of our clients in Miami, who lives in a luxury high-rise, was able to substantiate over $200,000 per year in tax-free rental income using this approach.

The Augusta Rule requires careful planning and proper documentation, but when executed correctly, it can create substantial tax savings.

Backdoor Roth Conversions

I have to admit it, the term "Backdoor Roth" sounds shady. In my early days as a CPA, I thought that anytime you converted from a traditional IRA to a Roth IRA, it was always taxable. But that's not true. After some studying and working with great tax attorneys, I realized this is a legit deal, and it's powerful.

There is a way to fund that traditional IRA, intentionally take it as a non-deductible contribution, and then immediately switch it to a Roth and do it in a tax-free way.

Because this one has the potential for significant tax savings, I've written an entire chapter to go into more detail.

Business Tax Credits

There is a lot of bang in this little textbook paragraph. We're talking about the hidden treasure chest known as business tax credits. When it comes to business taxes, credits are some of the most valuable tools available — they reduce your tax bill dollar for dollar. And there are a *lot* of them.

In fact, the IRS lists around 50 different business tax credits, ranging from general business and investment credits to very specific ones like:

- Work Opportunity Credit (for hiring employees from certain groups)
- Research & Development (R&D) Credit
- Low-Income Housing Credit
- Orphan Drug Credit
- Renewable Energy Credits (solar, wind, electric vehicles, and more)

Other valuable credits business owners often overlook include:

- Employer credit for paid family and medical leave
- Credit for small employer health insurance premiums
- Credit for employer-provided childcare facilities and services
- Credit for small employer pension plan startups
- Energy-efficient building and home credits

The takeaway here is this: you may be leaving money on the table. With dozens of available credits, each with its own rules and qualifications, the key is working with a CPA who actively reviews these opportunities for your business.

Capital Gains and Losses

Managing capital gains isn't just about reporting numbers — it's about strategic timing and coordination.

A few key areas where the right CPA makes all the difference:

- Understanding how to net capital gains and losses correctly
- Navigating the wash sale rules so losses aren't disallowed
- Coordinating tax strategy with your financial advisor to align with your investment plan

Here's where it gets powerful: under current tax law, long-term capital gains are taxed at 0%, 15%, or 20% depending on your taxable income. With careful planning, we can sometimes create opportunities to recognize gains in a year where your income is low enough to qualify for the 0% rate.

At Sarah Jones, CPA, we work with clients to identify those windows — helping them capture gains at the lowest possible tax cost.

Child IRA

An IRA for your child is one of the most powerful long-term wealth strategies — and a cornerstone of building a *Tax Free Millionaire*.

Here's how it works:

- For 2025, you can contribute up to $7,000 to your child's IRA (as long as they have earned income).
- You can choose a Traditional IRA or a Roth IRA:
    - Traditional IRA: contributions may be tax-deductible now, but withdrawals in retirement are taxable.
    - Roth IRA: contributions are made with after-tax dollars, but all future qualified withdrawals are tax free.

From experience, **99.9% of the time I recommend the Roth IRA route**. It's an extraordinary way to let compounding work for decades, ultimately helping your child build a tax-free retirement nest egg.

We'll go deeper into the *Tax Free Millionaire* strategy later, and I'll walk you through the exact steps in the online workbook — but this simple move is where it all begins.

Child Tax Credits

We all know our kids are a blessing — but they can also be expensive! Fortunately, the Child Tax Credit helps take a little pressure off.

For 2025, you may be eligible for up to $2,200 per child who is 17 or younger.

A few important notes:

- The credit is per child, making it especially valuable for larger families.
- Income limits apply — the credit begins to phase out as income rises.
- This is a credit, not just a deduction, meaning it reduces your tax bill dollar-for-dollar.

It's a simple but powerful way to put some money back in your pocket while raising your family.

Cost Basis Setup

Under IRS Code Section 1014, when someone passes away, the cost basis of most inherited assets (like stocks, real estate, or other investments) is automatically "stepped up" to the asset's fair market value on the date of death. This means your heirs won't owe capital gains tax on the appreciation that occurred during your lifetime—it essentially resets the clock. That can be a powerful tool in estate and succession planning, helping families preserve and transfer wealth more efficiently. At Sarah Jones, CPA, we guide clients through this process to maximize the benefits of this step-up in basis.

A similar concept applies with charitable donations. If you donate appreciated property, you can often deduct the fair market value—not just what you originally paid. For example, if you bought an asset for $25 and it's now worth $50, donating it may allow you to claim the full $50 deduction under current tax law. This not only supports causes you care about, but also provides a significant tax advantage.

Cost Segregation

For real estate investors, a cost segregation study can be a powerful tax strategy. Normally, residential rental properties are depreciated over 27.5 years and commercial properties over 39 years. But with a cost segregation study—performed by an engineering firm in compliance with IRS rules—your property is broken down into individual components such as HVAC systems, plumbing, roofing, and more.

This allows certain parts of the property to be depreciated over much shorter timeframes, unlocking significant accelerated depreciation. In years with 100% bonus depreciation (like this year), that can mean writing off a large portion of your property's value immediately, creating substantial tax savings and improving cash flow.

Crypto Loss Harvesting

Crypto is everywhere right now—and so are the tax questions that come with it. Many of our clients are coming to us for strategy on their crypto, which is taxed very similarly to capital gains and losses. That means every trade, sale, or conversion can have tax implications.

At **Sarah Jones, CPA**, we work closely with your financial advisor and review your exchange reports—whether from Coinbase or another platform—to make sure nothing is overlooked. If you have strategic losses, you can offset some gains. This is all about looking at where you are holistically— your entire financial picture, what gains you have, what losses you have—and then pairing it with strategies to lower your income. In some cases, if we manage the numbers carefully, we can even reduce or eliminate capital gains tax altogether.

Deferred Comp Plans

Deferred compensation plans are very powerful, especially for some of our business owners. There are many different deferred compensation plans, but the theory behind them is you're putting away money for your retirement. They are pre-tax dollars, which means you get a tax deduction for them.

If you're a business owner, some of these can be amped up and allow you to contribute huge amounts of money and, if you have employees, fund these for your employees as well and get an additional tax write-off. Make sure you are working with a qualified person to see which plan gives you the most bang for your tax buck.

There is a lot to go into with deferred compensation plans. We do a deep dive on these plans in our *Tax Free Millionaire* course, in our workbooks, and in our strategic setups with our clients.

Dependent Care Credit & FSA

If you're paying for child or dependent care so you can work, look for work, or attend school, tax savings may be available. Beginning in 2026 under the *One Big Beautiful Bill*, families can contribute up to $7,500 per household each year to a dependent care FSA ($3,750 if married filing separately).

The credit applies to qualifying expenses up to $3,000 for one dependent or $6,000 for two or more. Dependents must be under age 13, or unable to care for themselves due to physical or mental limitations. The credit is non-refundable—so while it can reduce your tax bill, it won't create a refund if you owe nothing.

Depreciation (Bonus and section 179)

Depreciation is one of the most powerful tax tools available to business owners. There are two main methods to know: bonus depreciation and Section 179 expensing.

- **Bonus depreciation** allows you to deduct a percentage of the cost of eligible property in the year it's placed in service. In recent years that percentage has shifted, but current law once again allows for 100% bonus depreciation. This means you may be able to write off the full cost of qualifying assets immediately.

- **Section 179** also allows for a full deduction of the purchase price, but it comes with rules: the asset must be used at least 50% for business, and there are annual deduction limits.

The key difference is that bonus depreciation has no dollar limit and can apply more flexibly, while Section 179 is capped and requires careful tracking. Both strategies can be very beneficial, but they also come with recapture rules—so it's important to only depreciate assets you plan to keep.

At **Sarah Jones, CPA**, we help you choose the best approach and integrate it into your overall tax strategy.

Dining and Food Optimization

There's a lot to unpack when it comes to meal deductions—and really, any tax write-offs. The key is making sure your books are accurate, and expenses are classified properly. That's where real savings happen.

Here's how meals typically break down:

- **100% deductible:** Certain business-related meals (for example, provided at company events).
- **50% deductible:** Most standard business meals with clients, prospects, or while traveling.
- **0% deductible:** Meals that don't meet IRS guidelines.

At Sarah Jones, CPA, we do a deep dive into your books, walking you through this process in the *Tax Free Millionaire* workbook and our courses. The goal is simple: to make sure you're getting the maximum benefit from every allowable write-off. Too many people leave money on the table (pun intended)—we help make sure that's not you.

Entity Selection

Keeping it really brief here because we could talk about entity selection and strategy for an entire book.

The bottom line is you need to start with your end result. What's your goal? A CPA who knows tax planning and tax strategy will help reverse engineer that into your operating and entity setup to make sure you're getting the most bang for your tax buck, not only in the short run but also in the long run, depending on your long-term goals and exit plans.

Entity selection and strategy is by far the first thing I look at with clients because it's the foundation for everything else. It's also a huge part of the *Tax Free Millionaire* lifestyle with our workbook and courses. This honestly is the number one strategy—the biggest bang for your tax buck—and it starts with making sure you're set up properly.

Health Insurance and Premiums

Health insurance deductions can be tricky because the rules depend on your business structure and ownership. Getting this right can mean big savings, but it has to be handled carefully.

- **S Corporations:** If you're a more-than-2% shareholder, health insurance premiums can't simply be deducted by the company. If they are paid, they're generally treated as taxable income to you.
- **C Corporations:** A C Corp can deduct health insurance premiums for employees, including owners—but whether a C corps structure makes sense overall depends on your bigger tax picture.
- **Other Options:** Tools like an accountable plan or reimbursements can create opportunities for additional write-offs, but they need to be set up correctly.

Handled the right way, health insurance and premiums can be a powerful part of your tax strategy. That's why we walk clients through this step-by-step in the *Tax Free Millionaire* System to make sure they get maximum benefit without creating problems down the road.

HSA

HSA accounts or a Health Savings Account is a great strategy. For 2025, you can contribute up to $4,300 for an individual or up to $8,550 for a family. If you are over the age of 55, you have a catch-up contribution and can put in an additional $1,000. This is not a use-it-or-lose-it account; it can accumulate over time, you can invest it, and those earnings are tax free. You also get a deduction for the money that you're putting into your HSA. It's a great strategy.

Itemized Deductions

Itemized deduction strategy is all about maximizing the impact in any given tax year. In 2025, President Trump signed into law the One Big Beautiful Bill, which had a big impact on several tax laws. As a business owner, (and even as a CPA) it was a lot of change all at once. Of course, Sarah Jones CPA has you covered at taxtrumponomics.com with a full onslaught of resources to help you navigate all this change.

Itemized deductions include charitable contributions, potential medical expenses, state and local taxes, mortgage interest, and similar expenses. If and when you have these expenses, it may make sense to pay some of them early or delay them, depending on what your taxable income will look like.

It's somewhat similar to windfall planning. Having a good CPA on your side to help you strategically get the most out of your itemized deductions is something we do here, and it's part of our *Tax Free Millionaire* course.

Late C Corp Election

There is a lot to unpack here. A **late C Corp election** is a strategy that could make sense if you initially missed the deadline to elect C corporation status. This is a complex decision that depends on your goals, but here's a high-level overview:

- You can file a **late election** using **Form 8832** if it's within **3 years plus 75 days** of your intended effective date.

You'll need to show reasonable cause, and there is IRS guidance (Revenue Procedure) that allows this.

- From a tax perspective, late C Corp elections usually make sense in two situations:
    1. **Growing profits**—you want to retain earnings within the corporation for expansion or other business purposes.
    2. **Future sale plans**—if you plan to sell the business and qualify for Qualified Small Business Stock (QSBS)under Section 1202, you could exclude up to $10 million or 10x your basis from capital gains taxes.

It's important to note that C Corps are generally double-taxed, so the structure isn't right for everyone. If your long-term plan includes going public, a C Corp is required. If your goal is a strategic sale, working with a CPA can help determine if the late C Corp election positions you to maximize benefits like the Section 1202 exclusion.

At **Sarah Jones, CPA**, we guide clients through these decisions, making sure your corporate structure aligns with your business and personal financial goals.

Late S Corp Election

If you spend any amount of time on TikTok and Instagram, you've heard all about the S corporation election. Let me begin by saying social media is not the most reliable way to get your tax education. But one thing they have gotten right, an S Corp is great for tax savings. However, it absolutely can be disastrous if it's not for the right person. You need to make sure that you're having that conversation about entity selection with a trained professional.

But let's go through a late S corps election to see if it makes sense for you. If you missed the deadline to elect S corporation status, a late S Corp election may still be possible—and could provide significant tax benefits. Here's what you need to know:

- You have up to 3 years plus 75 days after your intended effective date to file, as long as you meet IRS criteria.
- Requirements include:
  - You intended to be an S Corp but failed to submit Form 2553.
  - You can show reasonable cause for the missed deadline.
  - All shareholders must approve the election.
  - Your filing must reference an IRS Revenue Procedure supporting the reasonable cause.

An S Corp election helps reduce self-employment taxes. You still pay yourself a reasonable salary (with payroll taxes), but profits beyond that salary are generally not subject to self-employment tax. And for many business owners, this structure can lead to substantial tax savings over time.

Life Insurance Strategies

In this introductory phase, we do not have enough time to go through all the life insurance strategies. Because I promised to shoot straight with you, I will tell you I used to assume that you just need term insurance and invest the rest, which I now fully understand is awful advice for a well-diversified business owner.

Life insurance can give amazing diversification and an effective use of funds. You can become your own banker. Some cases depend on the setup, the intent, and the beneficiaries, but sometimes life insurance can even be tax deductible.

The biggest thing is you need to work with a CPA who understands life insurance and can help you through this. There is a huge opportunity here for business owners.

Lifetime Learning Credit

Here's another one for our students, the Lifetime Learning Credit. Under current tax law, this credit is up to $2,000 per return, not per student. So if you have five students on your return, it would actually only be $400 per student. The credit percentage is 20% of the first $10,000 in qualified educational expenses.

Here's where it differs from the American Opportunity Credit: this is not only for the first four years. You can use it for undergraduate, graduate, professional degree courses, and *even courses to improve your job skills*. It is available to both part-time and full-time students and can be claimed every year, with no limit on the number of years.

However, it is not refundable, meaning it can reduce your tax liability to zero but can't result in a refund if no tax is owed. It covers tuition and fees, and it can cover course-related expenses if they are required for enrollment and attendance, including books and supplies purchased from the institution as a condition of enrollment.

Long Term Rentals

We love working with our real estate clients because long-term rental properties are a powerful way to diversify your wealth and build long-term financial security—often with significant tax advantages.

If you're renting out a property year after year, there are several strategies that can enhance your tax position:

- **Cost segregation studies:** Particularly valuable for commercial properties or higher-end residential rentals, this strategy allows you to accelerate depreciation on components of the property.
- **Bonus depreciation:** Depending on your income level, bonus depreciation can help offset taxable income and improve cash flow.
- **Other income strategies:** Rentals can open doors to additional deductions and planning opportunities.

We cover these strategies in depth in our course, but the takeaway is simple: long-term rentals can be a win-win—helping you grow wealth over time while taking advantage of smart, tax-efficient strategies.

Low Income Housing Tax Credit

There's a lot to unpack here, but this one can be incredibly powerful for the right client. The Low-Income Housing Tax Credit, created under the Tax Reform Act of 1986 and codified in Section 42 of the Internal Revenue Code, provides developers with a dollar-for-dollar tax credit over a 10-year period. In return, they commit to offering housing that meets specific affordability requirements.

In simple terms, it's a win-win: you're supporting the creation of much-needed affordable housing, and the IRS rewards you with significant tax incentives. For certain clients, this strategy can be a key part of wealth-building and tax planning. For the right investor, it can be both impactful and highly beneficial.

Medical Expense Optimization

Like all of our other optimization strategies, this one is about being intentional, starting with your end goal in mind, then reverse engineering it to make sure you're getting the most bang for your tax buck.

- **For individuals:** Medical expenses are deducted on Schedule A, but only the portion that exceeds a certain percentage of your income counts. That's why we often look at ways to "bunch" expenses into a single year, so you cross that threshold and maximize your deduction.
- **For business owners (C Corp shareholders, for example):** There may be opportunities to structure medical expense reimbursements in a tax-efficient way. We also consider strategies like pairing this with a Health Savings Account (HSA) to stretch the benefits even further.

At the end of the day, it's all about optimization—finding the right timing and approach so your medical expenses work as hard for you as possible in your tax plan.

Net Investment Tax Minimization

A lot of people don't hear about the 3.8% Net Investment Income Tax (NIIT) until they see it on their tax return—often with surprise. But with planning, there are ways to minimize its impact.

What it applies to:
- Interest, dividends, and capital gains
- Passive rental income
- Royalties
- Passive income from partnerships or S corps
- Certain annuities and trust income

Strategies to reduce exposure:
- Spread gains over multiple years (for example, through installment sales)
- Harvest gains in years when your modified adjusted gross income is under the threshold
- Donate appreciated securities, or use tools like charitable remainder trusts or donor-advised funds
- Qualify as a real estate professional, which can exempt rental income
- Group passive activities under IRS rules to shift income from passive to active, which avoids NIIT

The bottom line: if your CPA tells you, "It is what it is," that's not the whole story. With the right strategies and planning, you can hedge against NIIT and potentially save significantly. At Sarah Jones, CPA, we make sure our clients know their options.

Optimizing Write-Offs

Let's talk about optimizing your write-offs. What does that really mean? It's not just about tracking receipts—it's about working with a CPA who actually digs into your books, keeps the bookkeeping clean, and makes sure every expense is coded properly. And here's the kicker: it's not just about compliance with IRS rules; it's about using the rules strategically so you're getting the biggest bang for your tax buck.

I can't tell you how many clients come to me after years with another CPA, and we find thousands in savings just by cleaning up and optimizing their write-offs. Honestly, it's low-hanging fruit. It's not even advanced strategy—it's simply making sure you're not leaving money on the table.

Passive Real Estate Losses and Strategies

For all of our real estate buddies out there, listen, I love real estate. You're not only building long-term wealth and watching properties appreciate, but you're also creating mailbox money with rental income *and* unlocking some big tax deductions.

Here's the deal: under IRS Code Section 469, passive real estate losses can only offset passive income. So if you've got a loss, great—it can cancel out passive gains. But here's where I push clients to think bigger: are you truly "passive," or is there a path to qualify as **active** under the tax code? Because if you can meet the test for material participation—maybe even qualify as a real estate professional—suddenly those losses can offset **active income**, which is a game changer.

There are a couple of key rules here:

- If your adjusted gross income is low enough, you can use the $25,000 rental real estate exception to offset active income—but that phases out quickly.
- Beyond that, we look at things like cost segregation studies and bonus depreciation to supercharge your deductions and maximize those losses.

Bottom line: for clients with a lot of passive income, passive real estate losses can be incredibly powerful. The trick is knowing how to use them strategically.

Paying Your Family

There is not a week that goes by that I do not have a client or a potential client asking me, "Hey, how can I pay my family? I saw on Facebook that I could pay my kids. Is this legitimate?" Absolutely. Can you get in trouble if you do it wrong? Abso-freaking-lutely.

You have to have a CPA who understands tax code—what you can and can't do. Because here's the thing: depending on how you're set up, what you can and can't do is different. You cannot just put your kids on payroll. They have to actually do work. You have to substantiate their work. It has to be legitimate.

Is this a great strategy? A thousand percent. Do we help clients do this every week? Absolutely. But you have to be able to substantiate everything you're doing to withstand an audit, and that's why you need a great CPA.

PIG Vs PALL

Let's talk about PIG versus PALL. Look, I'm from Texas, and for some reason this sounds like it's a credit for ranchers. But what this is talking about, PIG stands for passive income generator. PALL stands for passive activity loss, and really, they are two sides of the same coin. And it all goes under the passive activity loss rules under IRC 469.

Now, this really comes into play with our real estate investors and those who have limited partnerships in companies.

Why does it matter? You can use passive losses, or PALLs, to offset passive incomes, PIGs. Therefore, you can reduce or even eliminate your taxable income.

Here's the thing: at S-J-C-P-A, (just adding in my own acronyms), we work with our clients year-round because you want to see how your passive incomes are doing, your PIGs—versus your PALLs, your passive losses. And if we have any strategy that we can do to offset and eliminate taxable income in any given year, that's the key here. And it can be a huge, huge opportunity for some of our business owners that operate in passive ways.

QSBS Exclusions

I love the QSBS exclusion. Qualified Small Business Stock under Revenue Code 1202 is **extremely powerful** for business owners. It lets you exclude up to 100% of capital gains from the sale of QSBS from federal income tax, as long as a few key requirements are met.

Here's the biggest thing to understand: it has to be stock issued by a C corporation. If you're eligible, the gain on the sale of that stock can be partially—or entirely—tax free. The exclusion limit is the greater of $10 million or 10 times your basis in the stock, and you do need to hold it for at least five years.

And here's the kicker—you're also shielded from the 3.8% net investment income tax. That pesky tax doesn't apply here. Huge, huge opportunity.

As a Certified Exit Planning Advisor, I always say—you start with the end goal. If I know my client is building their business to sell (and really, if you're not, what are you even doing?), then this strategy can be a game changer. It can literally save you **hundreds of thousands of dollars** in federal taxes.

Qualified Charitable Contributions

A little complex, but I wanna give you a summary—qualified charitable contribution. If you are 70 and a half or older, and you have required minimum distributions, if you don't want the tax implication of that, you can gift away to a qualified public charity.

As of 2025, you can give up to $105,000 per year—that's a huge way to give back. Maybe it's to your church, your favorite cause, or your favorite school. And here's the best part: you can do it without triggering gift tax implications.

For my higher-net-worth clients, this can also be a powerful estate planning tool. If estate tax is on your radar, using this exclusion strategically can make a massive difference. It's generous giving that also helps you manage your tax picture.

Qualified Opportunity Zone

Qualified Opportunity Zone, for the right investor, this is a powerful tool. It was created under the Tax Cuts and Jobs Act of 2017. It offers capital gains tax deferral, reduction, and honestly a potential elimination if you invest in a QOF—a qualified opportunity fund.

A lot goes into this. You have to work with a good CPA. A lot of times we even bring in a really good real estate attorney to make sure that everything is absolutely buttoned up. There are certain deadlines you have to meet, similar to a 1031 exchange.

Here's the thing—you can also couple this or layer this with a 1031 exchange exit. You can couple this with an installment sale to spread out your entry, or you can create your own qualified opportunity fund to control the investments in compliance. You can also layer this with cost segregation and bonus depreciation, and you can potentially exit tax free using basis step-up.

I know this sounds like a lot, and it is. But know that we've got your back. We work with these clients all the time, and it's really a great strategy to use.

Residential Clean Energy Credits

Residential Clean Energy Credits—quick story. We moved into our house, and it was a new street, so there were tons of salesmen coming to our doors and knocking. I answered the door, and one guy said, "Ma'am, I've got a good thing for you. I'm gonna save you $15,000 on your taxes." And I said, "Well, what you don't know is that I'm a CPA who specializes in tax planning, and you're full of crap."

Here's the thing—clean energy credits are great, but do not sign up for something just to get a tax credit. It never makes sense to spend money just to get a fraction of it back as a credit. Now, if it's something you were going to do anyway, absolutely, it makes sense, but outside of that, it never makes sense.

So here's the deal on the Residential Clean Energy Credit. You can use it for things like solar panels, solar water heaters, geothermal heat pumps, small wind turbines, fuel cell systems, and battery storage.

For 2022 to 2032, the credit is 30%. After that, it's going to stair-step down. There's no dollar cap for most systems except for fuel cells. This is a non-refundable credit, meaning it can reduce your tax bill to zero, but it will not generate a refund.

To qualify for the Residential Clean Energy Credit here are a few rules:

- Must be for your primary or secondary U.S. residence (rental properties don't qualify)
- Applies to both existing homes and new construction
- Covers more than just panels: equipment, labor, on-site prep, permitting, inspection fees, and battery storage
- The credit must be claimed in the year the system is installed
- If your credit is larger than your tax liability, the unused portion carries forward to future tax years

Roth 401K

The Roth 401(k) is a powerful combination. It couples tax-free growth, higher contribution limits, and no income restrictions, which makes it an attractive option for young people, those who want future tax-free income, and high earners.

So, what are the key benefits of a Roth 401(k)?

- First, tax-free withdrawals at retirement.
- Second, high contribution limits. For 2025, you can contribute up to $23,500, plus there's a catch-up provision of $7,500 if you're over 50. That means you could put away up to $31,000. And if you're 60-63, you can contribute $34,750.
- No income limits.
- You can also potentially get employer matches, and if you're a business owner offering this, it's a tax write-off that decreases your taxable income.

It's a no-brainer. This is a huge, huge thing, and it aligns perfectly with our *Tax Free Millionaire* lifestyle that we teach you through our course, our books, our workbook, and our strategy sessions.

Roth IRA

Let's be honest—the Roth IRA does not give you a tax benefit the year you contribute. But—and this is a huge but—it is the superstar, the mamma-jamma, the foundation of the *Tax Free Millionaire* lifestyle.

Why? Because the Roth IRA gives you incredible tax advantages, flexibility, and long-term benefits. It creates tax-free retirement wealth, which is especially powerful for younger investors. It's a total game changer.

You don't get the upfront deduction, but your money grows tax free. And when you hit retirement, all of your qualified withdrawals are tax free. That includes your earnings. If you're 59½ or older and have held the account for at least five years, those withdrawals are 100% tax free.

I've written an entire chapter on the benefits of the Roth IRA.

Sale of Home

Sale of a home is sometimes the biggest sale that some of our clients ever face, and it can be a stressful time.

Under current tax law, you have an exclusion of $250,000 per taxpayer—so $250,000 if you're single or if you're married, up to $500,000 collectively together of capital gain exclusion.

We've had a lot of clients that sold a home in California and moved out here to Texas. You want to make sure you're getting every single credit available from that. You need to make sure that you have somebody looking at the closing documents, and you're taking all the closing expenses. You want to make sure that you're getting credit for anything that you have done improvement-wise because those expenses may have increased your basis.

We've gone through this with a lot of our clients from California and saved them thousands of dollars on the sale of their home. You want to make sure that if you sell your home, you don't just look at the exclusion, but that you're actually optimizing and looking and making sure you're not leaving anything on the table.

Schedule C Optimization

Schedule C is for our small business owners. It is for income and losses from a business.

What do I mean by optimization? Just like the couple of other sections we've had, it's making sure you have a trusted advisor who understands tax code, who understands tax planning, walking alongside you and making sure that you're getting the biggest deductions allowable under Internal Revenue Code, AKA the IRC.

Looking at all of those expense categories, are you quantifying all of that? What I find is a lot of our Schedule C business owners are just starting out and maybe they don't have QuickBooks, maybe they haven't reconciled monthly, and maybe they're just kind of pulling things up. What really makes sense is to sit down with our team, go through those bank statements, and get every single deduction.

I'll give you a quick example. I had a client—and actually still a client many years later. He had a couple of gym franchises, and he had a 1099 issued to him that he would take to his CPA. His CPA did not optimize his Schedule C, and when he came to me, I asked for his business bank account statements. We actually did his bookkeeping. I saved him hundreds of thousands of dollars in tax because his CPA was not taking any of his business deductions. The client didn't understand that he was supposed to submit all of this stuff to his CPA. The CPA was not doing the due diligence to ask for those deductions, and he overpaid by potentially hundreds of thousands of dollars. I don't want that to happen to you. So work with a CPA who will optimize your Schedule C.

Self-Directed Investment and Retirement Funds

Self-directed investing. I love this strategy for my clients who like to be in charge. They understand what they are doing, and they like taking risks. Oh, it's a double punch.

The tax advantages are, of course, if you're in a self-directed IRA, these are going to grow tax deferred. If it's self-directed, you have the potential for higher returns. If you have niche knowledge, like for example, if real estate is your jam or startups or IT, you can leverage your expertise in the market to get an above-average return coupled with a tax-advantageous landscape.

You can diversify beyond the public markets and really align with your personal values and goals. I really enjoy working with our clients who do self-directed investing because they're typically very dialed in on their strategy and typically are self-motivated. And of course, we come alongside them and make sure we get the biggest bang for their tax buck.

Short Term Rentals

We're getting into one of my favorite strategies for short-term rentals.

First of all, what is short-term rentals? As per the IRS, it needs to be that the average guest stay is seven days or fewer. These are rental activities, but they're non-passive. They're essential for maximizing deductions. You can reduce your taxable income while complying with IRS rules. If you operate, for example, an Airbnb, VRBO, or similar property, you can get aggressive tax benefits.

Here's the big thing—it gives you the ability to offset W2 income as long as we structure it properly, and that's really important. You have to materially participate in your short-term rentals, meaning you cannot be passive. As long as you can do that, we can offset W2 or other business income.

So how do you qualify? You have to meet one of the following: either 500 hours of participation, you're the only person substantially involved, or you have 100 hours or more than any other person. You need to work with a CPA who understands these rules, can help you walk through this, and help you substantiate it if you get audited.

You can couple this with depreciation and cost segregation studies. This can become very powerful to offset income for those people. We can even combine it with the real estate professional status, which means you can remain non-passive without the real estate professional designation if you materially participate—a unique loophole with lots of powerful opportunities.

We actually have a course all about short-term rentals, which is included with our *Tax Free Millionaire* Lifestyle, our workbook, our courses, and our strategies. If you're not looking at this, you are missing out on some great potential write-offs.

Simple 401K

For our business owners, the simple 401k is a great way not only to increase the stickiness of your employees strengthen company culture, and help your employees build wealth, but it can also help you save a little bit in tax.

Simple 401k stands for a savings incentive match plan for employees. It's a retirement plan for small businesses with less than a hundred employees, and it's kind of a blend. There's tax-deferred growth, lower administrative cost and burdens, and immediate tax savings for both the employers and the employees.

- Salary deferrals reduce taxable income for both employees and the business owner
- 2025 contribution limits:
  - Under 50: $16,500
  - 50 or older: $21,000 (includes $3,500 catch-up)
  - A super catch-up for those 60-63
- Employer contributions are deductible—any matching contributions reduce business taxable income.
- Can be strategically used in high-income years or with bonuses to maximize tax benefits
- Double win-win: helps employees save for retirement while lowering your taxable income

Special Purpose Vehicle LLC

An S-P-V-L-L-C. If you're a millennial like me, that sounds like something from an Eminem rap song. If you know, you know. If you didn't get my joke, I'm sorry; I thought it was pretty funny!

All kidding aside, here's the thing about a Special Purpose Vehicle, LLC. It offers unique tax and liability benefits for investors and fund managers, specific to real estate, venture capital, joint ventures, and private equity. It's kind of used if you want to pull together investor funds, isolate some risk, and have a flexible structure for one-time deals.

You can really leverage these into your overall tax strategy. It depends on what you have going on. What I will say, and I think we could go down a rabbit hole here, is if you're involved with any of these things—real estate, private equity, venture capital, and joint ventures—this is something that Sarah Jones CPAs will look at. If it's a great fit for you, we might recommend an S-P-V-L-L-C for you. Attorneys will be involved with it, and it really can be a powerful structure that also has some liability benefits as well.

Start Up Costs

There's a lot of value in having a solid strategy in place for your startup. Here's what you need to know:

- **Startup and organizational costs (IRS Section 195):**
  - Deduct up to $5,000 in startup costs **and** $5,000 in organizational costs **in the first year**
  - Phased out if your total exceeds $50,000; remaining costs are amortized over 15 years

- **Timing matters:**
  - ○ Deductions apply when your business becomes active—when you officially start offering goods or services
  - ○ Strategically planning your start date (e.g., starting operations in 2025) can maximize deductions for that tax year
- **Capital expenditures vs. startup costs:**
  - ○ Equipment, vehicles, and improvements are capitalized, not deducted as startup costs
  - ○ Can be paired with bonus depreciation or Section 179 to write off faster—but only once the business is active
- **Work with a CPA:**
  - ○ Proper classification of startup costs, organizational costs, capital assets, and operating expenses is key
  - ○ Proper planning can lead to substantial savings and ensure you get the biggest bang for your tax buck

Tax Loss Harvesting

This is something that I feel like is so misunderstood and is always overlooked. It's really important you have a CPA who is either also your tax advisor or your financial advisor, or is willing to meet with your financial advisor. S-J-C-P-A, we work with our financial advisors year-round because if there is synergy here, it is a huge value add for the client.

Most people know you can have a net loss of up to $3,000 to offset ordinary income every year if your losses exceed your gains. But here's the thing. Let's say that you have $50,000 of gains. Tax loss harvesting works to go to your portfolio, see what the losers are, and intentionally sell those to offset that gain.

I have so many clients who come to me and say, "Oh, I didn't realize I was gonna have this $100,000 capital gain. My financial advisor didn't tell me this." This is why it's so crucial. Get with a CPA who understands that you can go harvest some losses to offset some of these gains, and a CPA that's willing to work with your financial advisor. It could save you hundreds of thousands of dollars over your investing life.

Traditional 401K

Traditional 401k. There are some tax benefits for both the employee and the employer.

For 2025, the limit is $23,500. If you're over the age of 50, you have a catch up contribution, and you can contribute up to $31,000.

Everything that you put into these traditional plans are tax deferred, meaning if you had a hundred thousand dollars of income, and you put in $23,000, you now have taxable income of only $67,000.

The same thing applies for the employer. If you do matching, which is a great contribution for employee satisfaction, to keep people sticky for your firm, it is tax deductible. It's a win-win for both.

Travel Optimization

This is one of my favorite little strategies to really help business owners specifically take some fun stuff, legitimate travel deductions, and optimize this.

Number one, before anything, you have to establish the travel as a primary business purpose. If I, for example, and I'm giving this example because it actually happened, am going to Orlando for Disney and there happens to be a CPA conference there, that's not tax deductible because my primary purpose was taking my family to Disney. But if my primary business purpose was going to a conference, and I happened to take my family to Disney, now again, I'm not going to write off my family's Disney trip, but everything else on that business trip can be deductible because I established the primary business purpose.

You want to plan your trip strategically. You can add personal days before or after without losing the full transportation deductions, but you need to work with a CPA.

What can be deductible? Airfare, travel bus, cars, lodging, your meals, rental cars, taxi, rideshare, internet, phone, trips, and bag fees. What is not deductible? Personal excursions, like if I choose to go do a city tour, that's not deductible. Family member expenses, unless they're employees, and this piggybacks onto hiring your kids and your spouse strategically.

You have to have solid documentation. If you travel outside of the U.S., we have different standards that we have to abide by, and honestly, they're a little bit more liberal. If you have international travel planned, make sure that you're working with a CPA that can navigate this and make sure you get the most bang for your tax buck.

Tuition Reduction Strategies

Number one: if your child can be strategically paid through the company in a tax-efficient way, and again—hint, work with Sarah Jones, CPA to do this in compliance—we can hire your kids and pay them for their tuition in a roundabout way, allowing you to write off their college tuition. Pretty slick, huh?

Number two: set up a formal education assistance program through your business. You can give up to $5,250 per employee for educational expenses, tax free to your employees. This is a great way to increase stickiness to your firm, your business, and improve employee satisfaction.

Job-related education deduction: if you're self-employed or own a business, you can deduct tuition as a business expense only if it maintains or improves the skills required in your current trade or business. It's not allowed if it's for a new career.

And then your last resort, 529 college plans. You get limited tax reduction here, but it's still strategic. Everything that goes into the 529 is tax free, and withdrawals for qualified educational expenses are also tax free.

If you're an employer, you can set up a tuition reimbursement program for employees. It can be for job-related education and still be deductible for the business. You can reimburse employees for this—it's a business expense for you, which decreases your taxable income, but it does become taxable to the employee, and there must be a clear connection to the business needs.

There's a lot going on with tuition reduction, and depending on your situation, we can make sure you get the biggest bang for your tax buck.

Windfall Planning

What does windfall planning even mean? It means you have something going on, and it's usually something really amazing, but there's some tax implications. Maybe you have an inheritance, or you're gonna get a distribution from a trust, you got some gambling winnings, you won the lottery, you have a huge sale of a business, or maybe some stock options, some type of legal settlement, or a large bonus.

So here's the thing—that's amazing—but without proper planning, these can push you into a much higher tax bracket and potentially trigger additional taxes like net investment tax and/or disqualify you from credits and deductions that you typically get to have.

When you work with a CPA—like Sarah Jones, CPA—there are some really powerful ways to manage and smooth out your tax bill. For example, we can look at strategies to spread income across multiple years, so you're not taxed all at once. In business or real estate deals, installment sales can be a great way to defer part of the gain and keep your taxable income lower in a given year. And if you have stock options, we can time the exercise and sales to align with years when your income is lower. The bottom line is this: with the right planning, you don't just accept the tax hit—you structure it so the taxes work in your favor.

There are so many ways we can handle your windfalls. We can do some charitable planning, maybe both immediate and long term. We can do donor-advised funds a charitable remainder trust, a qualified charitable distribution, maybe a private foundation if it makes sense. On the capital gains minimization, we can look at maybe some tax loss harvesting, use appreciated stocks for donations to get that step up in basis, and then we go into a whole other onslaught of tools with trust and estate planning tools: we can use some irrevocable trust to shift growth out of your estate to reduce that tax exposure, we can set up spousal lifetime access trusts, dynasty trusts, and gifting strategies.

Above and Beyond

All of the strategies listed above are workhorse strategies of the tax-industry. Still, you'd be surprised at the number of clients we bring on whose CPA and/or financial planner were not even utilizing the basics. In addition to all of the ABCs of Tax Credits, Sarah Jones, CPA utilizes these advanced tax-savings strategies as well.

- 1031 EXCHANGE
- 457 MARK TO MARKET FOR TRADERS
- 83B STOCK ELECTION
- ACTIVE REAL ESTATE PROFESSIONAL
- ACTIVE TRADER STATUS
- C CORP WITH UNLIMITED PASSIVE LOSS RESTRICTIONS
- CHARITABLE REMAINDER TRUST
- CHARITABLE GIFT FINANCING
- CHARITABLE HOLDING LLC
- CHARITABLE LEAD ANNUITY TRUST
- CHARITABLE LLC LIKE CRT USING DAF LIKE FOUNDATION, 1% EFF RATE
- CHARITABLE LLCS FOR SPECIFIC PLANNING
- CHARITABLE POOLED INCOME FUND
- CONSERVATION EASEMENT
- CRYPTO MINING AND STAKING
- DEFERRED SALES TRUST
- DELAWARE STATUTORY TRUSTS
- DONOR ADVISED FUND
- DYNASTY TRUST

- ECOMM SOFTWARE TECHNOLOGY LEVERAGE
- EMPLOYEE STOCK OPTIONS
- EXIT PLANNING STRATEGIES
- FAMILY OFFICE
- FILM DEBT FINANCING
- FILM DEDUCTION (IRC181)
- FINANCED BUSINESS INSURANCE
- GRANTOR RETAINED ANNUITY TRUST
- HEALTHCARE SOFTWARE RTU PROGRAM
- HEDGE FUND WITH 988, 757 AND 704B
- HISTORIC REHABILI-TATION TAX CREDITS
- LEVERAGED ASSET DONATIONS
- LEVERAGED CHARITABLE DONATIONS
- LEVERAGED TECHNOLOGY PURCHASE
- LIFE INSURANCE COST REDUCTION STRATEGIES
- LIFE INSURANCE STRATEGIES
- MEDICAL CHARITABLE DONATION
- NEW MARKETS TAX CREDIT
- OIL AND GAS
- OPPORTUNITY ZONES
- PRIVATE FAMILY FOUNDATION
- PRIVATE FOUNDATION
- PRIVATE FOUNDATIONS/ RMDS TO PRIVATE FOUNDATION
- RESTRICTED STOCK UNIT (RSU) PLANNING
- SMALL ADVANTAGE/ FRACTIONAL OWNERSHIP PROGRAM
- SOCIAL SECURITY PLANNING
- SOFTWARE INVEST-MENT PROJECTS
- STATE DOMICILE PLANNING

- STOCK REDEMPTION STRATEGY
- STRUCTURED INVESTMENT STRATEGY
- TAX ADVANTAGED HEDGE FUND INVESTMENTS
- TAX DOMICILE PLANNING
- TAX FREE (DOUBLE DIP) DEFINED BENEFIT PLAN STRATEGY
- VIRTUAL FAMILY OFFICE
- WEALTH EXCEL STRATEGY-BLUEPRINT

Your Next Step

We offer custom-built advanced and VIP strategies for our clients. And I think by now you know that Sarah Jones, CPA is a tax-planning machine. It's what we do best. If you read through this chapter (which to be clear is just the tip of the iceberg), and you thought, "Oh, we should be doing this," or "I wonder why we **aren't** doing this?" then visit us at www. taxfreemillionairesystem.com, and let's start working on getting you these savings.

Chapter 10
Meet the Superstar of *Tax Free Millionaire*

L et's talk about the most powerful, most often overlooked tool in the *Tax Free Millionaire* toolbox, the superstar that is the Roth IRA.

Now, this isn't some groundbreaking new strategy. The Roth IRA has been around for decades. But just because it's old doesn't mean it's outdated. In fact, when used correctly—especially in combination with smart tax planning—it can play a critical role in helping you build long-term, completely tax-free wealth.

Why the Roth IRA Matters

Unlike a traditional IRA, the Roth IRA doesn't give you a tax deduction upfront. Instead, you contribute after-tax dollars— and in exchange, your investment grows tax free and can be withdrawn tax free in retirement.

|

Let that sink in— tax-free *growth* and tax-free *withdrawals*. That's what makes the Roth so powerful.

In contrast, a traditional IRA works more like a 401(k). You may get a deduction for contributions (if you're under the income limits), but you'll pay taxes later when you pull that money out. It's not a bad option—but it's not the wealth accelerator the Roth can be.

Contribution Limits (2025)

As of 2025:

- You can contribute up to **$7,000** annually to a Roth IRA.
- If you're age 50 or older, you're allowed an additional **$1,000** catch-up contribution, for a total of **$8,000**.

So, if you're like my husband Phil—who qualifies for the catch-up—you've got a little extra room to grow.

What This Means For You

When you work with Sarah Jones, CPA, we include a *Tax Free Millionaire* Forecast as part of your personalized assessment. Based on your age and current financial situation, we'll project how much tax-free wealth you can accumulate using Roth strategies over your lifetime.

And here's the best part: this isn't money you necessarily have to come out of pocket to invest.

We often find that our clients are overpaying the IRS. Once we identify the overages, we redirect that wasted money and reallocate it—strategically—into vehicles like a Roth IRA. That's how you begin to build a truly tax-free legacy.

Roth IRA vs. Traditional IRA: Quick Recap		
	Roth IRA	**Traditional IRA**
Tax Deduction Now?	No	Yes (if under income limit)
Tax-Free Growth?	Yes	No
Tax-Free Withdrawals?	Yes	No
Required Distributions?	No (for owner)	Yes

We leverage the Roth IRA in our system wherever possible. Why? Because it allows you to set money aside today and withdraw it tomorrow with zero tax implications. That's the definition of smart planning.

The Spousal IRA

Let's talk about a simple, yet incredibly powerful—and also often overlooked—strategy: the Spousal IRA.

You may have heard of it, but most people don't fully grasp the opportunity it creates. It's one of those quiet loopholes that can radically shift your family's financial future when used intentionally.

How It Works

Here's the scenario: Tom works full time and earns a solid income. His wife Sarah stays home to raise their children. Under normal rules, Sarah wouldn't be eligible to contribute to an IRA because she doesn't have earned income.

But the IRS allows a special provision—the Spousal IRA—which lets a working spouse fund an IRA for their non-working spouse, as long as the couple files taxes jointly and meets certain income limits. This means Tom can fully fund an IRA for Sarah—even though she earns no income herself.

Let that sink in.

Tom can create a path for *both* of them to build long-term, tax-free wealth, even if only one of them earns income outside the home.

Creating Two *Tax Free Millionaires*

Now imagine Tom and Sarah are in their mid-twenties with two small kids. Tom contributes to both his and Sarah's Roth IRAs every year. Over time, both accounts grow—completely tax free.

And here's where it gets even more powerful. Let's say Tom is a business owner working with Sarah Jones, CPA. Through year-round tax strategy, we help him save 30% on his taxes. Instead of sending that money to the IRS, Tom reinvests it into *his family's future*—funding both Roth IRAs, building wealth for himself *and* for Sarah.

Sarah may never work a day outside the home. She may be raising children, fostering, volunteering, or leading in her community—but that doesn't mean she can't be a *Tax Free Millionaire*. Under current IRS guidelines, she absolutely can.

The Big Picture

This is what strategic tax planning is all about: taking dollars you were going to lose to taxes and using them to create lasting, generational wealth. With the right strategy, a single-income household can still create two financially independent, tax-free retirements.

So, if you're the "Tom" in your family—earning the income while your spouse manages the home—don't miss this opportunity. With the right CPA and the right plan, you can double your wealth-building potential. Let us guide you through it—step-by-step—and show you how to create not just one, but *two Tax Free Millionaires* in your family.

Backdoor Roth

I'll be honest—my personal favorite chapter in this book is where we talked about the mind shift needed to truly adopt the *Tax Free Millionaire* lifestyle. But if I had to guess which chapter *you*, the reader, will love most? It's probably this one.

Why? Because the Backdoor Roth IRA is one of the most powerful, misunderstood, and underutilized strategies in the entire tax code.

And I'll admit, there was a time, even as a CPA, when I misunderstood it too. Clients would bring it up, and I'd brush it off. "That's not real," I'd say. "You can't do that." But then I took a deeper dive, got the right education, and finally understood what was really going on.

And let me tell you—it's real, it's legal, and it's amazing.

What Is a Backdoor Roth IRA?

The Backdoor Roth IRA is designed for high-income earners—people who make too much money to contribute directly to a Roth IRA due to IRS income limits.

Here's how it works:

1. **Step One:** You contribute the maximum allowable amount to a traditional IRA.

   ° Normally, traditional IRA contributions are tax-deductible—but in this case, we don't take the deduction.

○ Instead, we file a special IRS form indicating that this is a non-deductible contribution on your tax returns.

2. **Step Two:** You convert the funds from your traditional IRA into a Roth IRA. That's it. It's a legal, IRS-compliant workaround to the income limits. You've effectively gone *through the back door* into a Roth IRA, even though your income technically disqualifies you.

Why Is This a Big Deal?

Because Roth IRAs are gold. Once the funds are inside your Roth, they grow tax free, and you can withdraw them tax free in retirement. So even if you earn well above the income limits, you can still use this strategy to build tax-free wealth.

And yes, you can do this for your spouse too. That means if you're a high-earning couple, you can double up on this strategy each year.

Example: Tom the Business Owner

Let's go back to our favorite example—Tom, the high-earning business owner. Tom is bringing in a couple million a year, well above the Roth IRA income limits. But because he works with Sarah Jones, CPA, here's what happens:

- He contributes the maximum to both his and his wife's traditional IRAs
- We file the correct tax form to report these as non-deductible contributions
- Then we immediately convert both accounts to Roth IRAs

Now Tom and his wife are building *Tax Free Millionaire* wealth—legally, strategically, and in full compliance with IRS rules.

The Key: Do It Right

Here's the most important thing to remember. You have to report it properly. If you don't file the form indicating that the traditional IRA contribution is non-deductible, this whole strategy falls apart—and you could owe unexpected taxes.

That's why it's critical to work with a CPA who understands how to implement this correctly. This is one of the simplest and most effective tools available, but it requires precision to execute.

Your Next Step

Depending on when you're reading this, tax laws may have changed. Visit www.taxfreemillionairesystem.com to get the most current information. You'll find affordable resources, current strategies, and access to our *Tax Free Millionaire* tools. Let's put your money to work.

Chapter 11

Leverage Your Kids

If we're going to talk about generational wealth, let's get real about what that actually looks like. It's not just leaving your kids a lump sum when you die. It's giving them the mindset, tools, and structures to build and sustain wealth long after you're gone. And one of the most powerful gifts you can give them? A head start. Not just in life—but in tax-free wealth building. So let's talk about how to strategically, legally, and proactively turn your children into *Tax Free Millionaires*. Yes, it's possible— and no, it doesn't take millions to get started. Just intention, planning, and the right strategy.

Part One: Can You Put Your Kids on Payroll?

If you're a business owner, you might be wondering: *Can I put my kids on payroll and get a tax deduction?*

The short answer? **Maybe.**

It all comes down to how your business is structured. Under current IRS rules, if your business is a:

- Single-member LLC, or
- Husband-and-wife partnership

...then yes—you can potentially put your children on payroll and deduct their wages *without* them having to pay income tax on that money (as long as total annual earnings fall under the standard deduction limit for the year).

But—and this is key—your kids must actually perform real, documentable work. This isn't a loophole to pay your 6-month-old $14,000 for being "featured in a Facebook post." The IRS expects that the work be **reasonable** for your business, and that means:

- Assigning age-appropriate tasks
- Keeping records of hours works and payments issued

Treat them like a real employee, because for tax purposes, they are one. Done right, this strategy can reduce your taxable income, keep more money in the family, and start your kids on the road to becoming true *Tax Free Millionaires.*

That's why you must work with a qualified CPA (a real one, not a self-proclaimed guru on TikTok) who understands how to do this correctly and compliantly.

Now, if you're an S Corporation or standard partnership, this loophole doesn't apply in the same way. You can still put your children on payroll, but you'll need to issue W-2s or 1099s, and regular tax rules will apply. Even then, it may still be worth doing—but you'll need a tax strategist to walk you through the best approach for your setup.

Part Two: Turning Your Kids Into *Tax Free Millionaires*

Here's where things get even more exciting.

If your child has earned income—whether from a part-time job, working in your business, or another legitimate source—you can fund a Roth IRA for them.

Let's break this down.

Imagine your 12-year-old helps out in your business, doing admin tasks or organizing files. Over the course of the year, they earn $7,000 in legitimate, documented income. You can use that income to fully fund a Roth IRA in their name.

That money will grow tax free. And when they're ready to use it in retirement, they'll be able to pull it out tax free as well.

This is the magic of compound interest paired with decades of time. If you help your kids start investing at 12, 14, or 16 years old, you're giving them a massive head start toward financial independence. You're literally changing their future—and potentially rewriting your family legacy.

Note: Check for updated One Big Beautiful Bill on the government website.

What We Offer

At Sarah Jones, CPA, we make this process simple. If you go through our *Tax Free Millionaire* Roadmap, we'll:

- Review your tax situation
- Identify savings opportunities
- Show you exactly how much wealth you and your family could build over time

We also provide tools, affordable resources, and calculators to help you forecast future growth and understand the long-term value of these decisions.

Your Next Step

Everyone wants their kids to succeed. As parents, we invest in their education, we drive them to events, we show up for the school plays.

But what about financial freedom?

Helping your children become *Tax Free Millionaires* isn't about spoiling them—it's about empowering them. It's about teaching them how to build and steward wealth wisely. And it starts with a simple strategy, executed well.

So if you're a parent, business owner, or both—this is your invitation to stop leaving tax-saving opportunities on the table and start building generational wealth on purpose.

I know it's at the end of every chapter, but it bears repeating: We have lots of resources to help you through all of these strategies. Scan the QR code in this book or visit www.taxfreemillionairesystem.com to get the latest tools and start your family's *Tax Free Millionaire* journey.

Chapter 12
Tale of Two Businesses

This is the Tale of our Two Business Owners where we bring it all together.

In Part One of this book, we've walked through what it means to live the *Tax Free Millionaire* lifestyle. We've covered why you need a strategic CPA, why traditional tax prep just isn't enough, and the hidden costs and long-term risks of flying blind. We've exposed the American Dream for what it really is, an invitation to debt, and revealed how to take control through proactive, powerful tax planning.

In Part Two, we gave you the solutions: tax-planning foundations and the ABCs of tax strategies and loopholes, and tools like the Roth IRA, the spousal IRA, the backdoor Roth, and how to leverage your kids for wealth creation. If you've read through all that—congrats. You've got everything you need to rewrite your financial future.

Now, let me re-introduce you to two familiar characters: **Tom** and **Kathy**. Their stories illustrate exactly why this work matters.

Meet Tom - The Teachable Business Owner

Tom is every CPA's dream client. He's coachable, open, and eager to grow. Tom owns an HVAC company pulling in around $5 million in annual revenue with strong net income. When he came to Sarah Jones, CPA, he'd never done formal tax planning. He'd worked with the same CPA for 20 years—a nice guy, but not a strategist. Every time Tom asked how he could stop giving so much of his money to the government. He was told, *"It is what it is."*

But Tom knew there had to be a better way.

We offered our *Tax Free Millionaire* Roadmap and immediately identified massive opportunities. First, we restructured his entity. That alone saved him around **25% annually** in taxes. Then, we implemented key strategies:

- A backdoor Roth IRA (since his income exceeded the contribution limits)
- A spousal IRA (his wife stayed home full-time)
- Payroll integration for his kids, who legitimately worked in his business
- Roth IRA contributions for those kids, leveraging compound interest from a young age

All legal. All strategic. All built with his unique goals in mind.

Tom is now on track to save $2.5 million in taxes over his lifetime and accumulate an estimated $6 million in tax-free wealth for himself, his wife, and his kids.

Let that sink in. $6 million in tax-free wealth. And, on top of that $6 million in tax free wealth, he also accumulated another $6.3 million in an investment account—funded entirely from his tax savings. Read that all again, $6 million in tax-free wealth, plus another $6.3 million in a brokerage account. That's a whopping $12.3 million in wealth built...All. From. Tax. Savings. Put another way, (just to make sure this is sinking in!) you can become a multimillionaire, simply by integrating the Tax Free Millionaire system and using the tax dollars you would have given to Uncle Sam, then putting them to work for you, your family, your future and your legacy. (I feel it's appropriate to enter a mic drop here. You're welcome.)

Now Meet Kathy - The Skeptic

Kathy also runs a successful business, earning roughly what Tom does. She came to our firm curious about tax planning, and we were happy to help. We showed her how we could save her nearly 27.5% annually in taxes and build a comprehensive *Tax Free Millionaire* strategy.

But once she realized this wasn't a part of her tax preparation, she lost interest.

She couldn't see real tax planning is a premium, a high-ROI service. And despite seeing the numbers and knowing the opportunity, she declined to invest in the process.

She walked away.

Based on our analysis, Kathy is on track to overpay the IRS by more than $2 **million** dollars during her lifetime. Even worse? If she had utilized the same strategies as Teachable Tom, she would have made over $7 million dollars in accumulated wealth, PLUS the $2 million dollars she paid in tax. That's a total of $9.2 million dollars in lost, tax-free growth and legacy wealth. All because she didn't see the value—or wasn't willing to shift her mindset with the *Tax Free Millionaire* Roadmap.

TAX FREE Millionaire

Sarah Jones CPA

| END AMOUNT | ADDITIONAL CONTRIBUTION | RETURN RATE | STARTING AMOUNT | INVESTMENT LENGTH |

Starting Amount	0
After	20 YEARS
Return Rate	12
Compound	ANNUALLY
Additional Contribution	7,000

Contribute at the ☐ beginning ☐ end

of each ☐ month ☐ year

Calculate

Results

End Balance	$564,891.15
Starting Amount	$0.00
Total Contributions	$140,000.00
Total Interest	$424,891.15

Accumulation Schedule

ANNUAL SCHEDULE   MONTHLY SCHEDULE

YEAR	DEPOSIT	INTEREST	ENDING BALANCE
1	$7,000.00	$840.00	$7,840.00
2	$7,000.00	$1,780.80	$16,620.80
3	$7,000.00	$2,834.50	$26,455.30
4	$7,000.00	$4,014.64	$37,469.93
5	$7,000.00	$5,336.39	$49,806.32
6	$7,000.00	$6,816.76	$63,623.08
7	$7,000.00	$8,474.77	$79,097.85
8	$7,000.00	$10,331.74	$96,429.59
9	$7,000.00	$12,411.55	$115,841.15
10	$7,000.00	$14,740.94	$137,582.08
11	$7,000.00	$17,349.85	$161,931.93
12	$7,000.00	$20,271.83	$189,203.76
13	$7,000.00	$23,544.45	$219,748.22
14	$7,000.00	$27,209.79	$253,958.00
15	$7,000.00	$31,314.96	$292,272.96
16	$7,000.00	$35,912.76	$335,185.72
17	$7,000.00	$41,062.29	$383,248.00
18	$7,000.00	$46,829.76	$437,077.77
19	$7,000.00	$53,289.33	$497,367.10
20	$7,000.00	$60,524.05	$564,891.15

INVESTMENT CALCULATOR

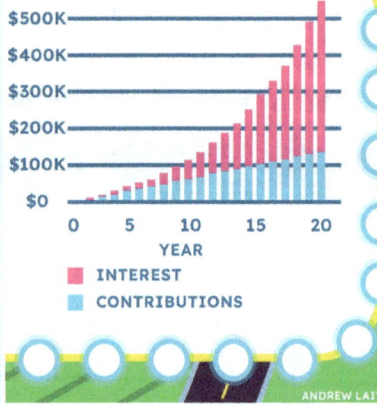

INTEREST
CONTRIBUTIONS

ANDREW LAITINEN

INVESTMENT CALCULATOR

| END AMOUNT | ADDITIONAL CONTRIBUTION | RETURN RATE | STARTING AMOUNT | INVESTMENT LENGTH |

Starting Amount `0`
After `40 YEARS`
Return Rate `12`
Compound `ANNUALLY`
Additional Contribution `7,000`

Contribute at the ☐ beginning ☐ end
of each ☐ month ☐ year

Calculate

Results

End Balance	$6,013,996.74
Starting Amount	$0.00
Total Contributions	$280,000.00
Total Interest	$5,733,996.74

Accumulation Schedule
ANNUAL SCHEDULE   MONTHLY SCHEDULE

YEAR	DEPOSIT	INTEREST	ENDING BALANCE	YEAR	DEPOSIT	INTEREST	ENDING BALANCE
1	$7,000.00	$840.00	$7,840.00	21	$7,000.00	$68,626.94	$640,518.09
2	$7,000.00	$1,780.80	$16,620.80	22	$7,000.00	$77,702.17	$725,220.26
3	$7,000.00	$2,834.50	$26,455.30	23	$7,000.00	$87,866.43	$820,086.69
4	$7,000.00	$4,014.64	$37,469.93	24	$7,000.00	$99,250.40	$926,337.09
5	$7,000.00	$5,336.39	$49,806.32	25	$7,000.00	$112,000.45	$1,045,337.54
6	$7,000.00	$6,816.76	$63,623.08	26	$7,000.00	$126,280.50	$1,178,618.05
7	$7,000.00	$8,474.77	$79,097.85	27	$7,000.00	$142,274.17	$1,327,892.21
8	$7,000.00	$10,331.74	$96,429.59	28	$7,000.00	$160,187.07	$1,495,079.28
9	$7,000.00	$12,411.55	$115,841.15	29	$7,000.00	$180,249.51	$1,682,328.79
10	$7,000.00	$14,740.94	$137,582.08	30	$7,000.00	$202,719.45	$1,892,048.25
11	$7,000.00	$17,349.85	$161,931.93	31	$7,000.00	$227,885.79	$2,126,934.03
12	$7,000.00	$20,271.83	$189,203.76	32	$7,000.00	$256,072.08	$2,390,006.12
13	$7,000.00	$23,544.45	$219,748.22	33	$7,000.00	$287,640.73	$2,684,646.85
14	$7,000.00	$27,209.79	$253,958.00	34	$7,000.00	$322,997.62	$3,014,644.48
15	$7,000.00	$31,314.96	$292,272.96	35	$7,000.00	$362,597.34	$3,384,241.81
16	$7,000.00	$35,912.76	$335,185.72	36	$7,000.00	$406,949.02	$3,798,190.83
17	$7,000.00	$41,062.29	$383,248.00	37	$7,000.00	$456,622.90	$4,261,813.73
18	$7,000.00	$46,829.76	$437,077.77	38	$7,000.00	$512,257.65	$4,781,071.38
19	$7,000.00	$53,289.33	$497,367.10	39	$7,000.00	$574,568.57	$5,362,639.94
20	$7,000.00	$60,524.05	$564,891.15	40	$7,000.00	$644,356.79	$6,013,996.74

TAX FREE Millionaire

Sarah Jones CPA

END AMOUNT	ADDITIONAL CONTRIBUTION	RETURN RATE	STARTING AMOUNT	INVESTMENT LENGTH

Starting Amount	0		
After	20 YEARS		
Return Rate	12		
Compound	ANNUALLY		
Additional Contribution	79,000		

Contribute at the ☐ beginning ☐ end

of each ☐ month ☐ year

Calculate

Results

End Balance	$6,375,200.11
Starting Amount	$0.00
Total Contributions	$1,580,000.00
Total Interest	$4,795,200.11

INVESTMENT CALCULATOR

Accumulation Schedule

ANNUAL SCHEDULE MONTHLY SCHEDULE

YEAR	DEPOSIT	INTEREST	ENDING BALANCE
1	$79,000.00	$9,480.00	$88,480.00
2	$79,000.00	$20,097.60	$187,577.60
3	$79,000.00	$31,989.31	$298,566.91
4	$79,000.00	$45,308.03	$422,874.94
5	$79,000.00	$60,224.99	$562,099.93
6	$79,000.00	$76,931.99	$718,031.93
7	$79,000.00	$95,643.83	$892,675.76
8	$79,000.00	$116,601.09	$1,088,276.85
9	$79,000.00	$140,073.22	$1,307,350.07
10	$79,000.00	$166,362.01	$1,552,712.08
11	$79,000.00	$195,805.45	$1,827,517.53
12	$79,000.00	$228,782.10	$2,135,299.63
13	$79,000.00	$265,715.96	$2,480,015.59
14	$79,000.00	$307,081.87	$2,866,097.46
15	$79,000.00	$353,411.69	$3,298,509.15
16	$79,000.00	$405,301.10	$3,782,810.25
17	$79,000.00	$463,417.23	$4,325,227.48
18	$79,000.00	$528,507.30	$4,932,734.78
19	$79,000.00	$601,408.17	$5,613,142.95
20	$79,000.00	$683,057.15	$6,375,200.11

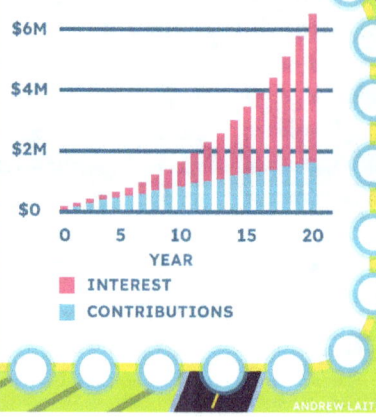

INTEREST
CONTRIBUTIONS

ANDREW LAITINEN

So ... Who Are You?

At this point, you've seen both paths. One leads to compounding wealth, tax freedom, and a legacy that lasts. The other leads to unnecessary tax bills, lost opportunity, and regret.

So ask yourself: **Are you a Tom—or are you a Kathy?**

Most of us would say "Tom," of course. The question is, will you actually take the steps it takes to be Tom?

We created the *Tax Free Millionaire* System for people just like you—business owners who are ready to stop surviving and start scaling. This isn't just a book. This is a movement. A mindset shift. A revolution in how you build and protect your wealth.

Your Next Step

Visit www.taxfreemillionairesystem.com. Learn about the *Tax Free Millionaire* Roadmap. We'll analyze your current situation, estimate how much you're overpaying the IRS, and show you what kind of tax-free wealth you could build for yourself, your spouse, and your kids.

This book was written in 2025. Tax law changes every year. Our website always has the latest updates, tools, and resources to keep you compliant and ahead of the curve.

So here's the challenge:

Be like Tom.

Take action.

Start now.

We can't wait to work with you.

Chapter 13

The Finish Line

We're almost at the finish line. And before you close this book, I want to shift gears and make sure everything we've covered clicks into place.

You've learned the *why*. You've seen the *how*. You've heard the stories. You've been given access to the tools, the strategies, and the mindset shift needed to rewrite your financial future. You've got the QR code below and the website—www. taxfreemillionairesystem.com—with tons of resources waiting for you.

But now, let's button it up. Let's talk about what it really takes to become a *Tax Free Millionaire*.

Step 1: Work With a Qualified Tax Planner

This is non-negotiable.

You need to work with a CPA or tax attorney who specializes in tax planning. Not someone who just files your returns once a year. Not a self-proclaimed tax guru on social media. You owe it to yourself—and your family—to partner with a licensed professional who knows how to design strategy, not just crunch numbers.

Every year you delay this, you're giving away money—*your money*—to the IRS, money that could have been building wealth for your future.

The first step with any good tax firm (including ours) is an analysis. We assess your current tax situation, look at your goals, and build a strategy that fits. If a CPA jumps straight into tactics without understanding your full picture, walk away. It's like hiring a personal trainer who throws you on a treadmill before asking about your health.

Good planning starts with clarity. It starts with a custom plan.

Step 2: Work With a Financial Advisor Who Understands the System

Next, you need a financial advisor who understands the *Tax Free Millionaire* System. Ideally, one who works *with* your CPA so the two can strategize together.

That's what Phil Jones and I do—we created this system, and we work side-by-side with our clients to bring it to life.

But if you already have an advisor you love, fantastic. Have them read this book. The strategies themselves aren't new. What *is* unique is how they're put together in one holistic, intentional, and strategic system.

And here's the thing—strategies only work if you implement them. That means opening the accounts, funding them regularly, and staying consistent. Skipping steps won't get you results. This is how real, lasting tax-free wealth is built—for you, your spouse, and your kids. It's not magic. It's disciplined action over time.

Step 3: Make It a Year-Round Commitment

One tax planning session a year won't cut it. You need ongoing, year-round tax strategy and updates. At Sarah Jones, CPA, we work with our clients throughout the year—checking in, adjusting strategies, forecasting results, and making sure every move is aligned with your long-term vision.

We're not just here to file. We're here to build.

Your Next Step

Your next step is to become a *Tax Free Millionaire*. It's simpler than you think:

1. **Get a tax-planning analysis** with a qualified CPA (for us, this is the *Tax Free Millionaire* Roadmap)
2. **Work with a financial advisor** who understands and supports your strategy.
3. **Leverage your tax savings** to fund tax-free wealth accounts.
4. **Stay consistent**—year after year—until the results compound into a legacy.

For business owners especially, this is a no-brainer. We'll likely save you **20–30% annually** on taxes. Then we'll take those savings and move them into the right accounts—Roth IRAs, backdoor Roths, spousal IRAs, custodial accounts for your kids.

We'll show you how to grow tax-free wealth, rewrite your family tree, and build a legacy that outlives you.

This is how it's done.

Chapter 14

Your Invitation

W e're almost at the end of *Tax Free Millionaire*, and this chapter is for those who are ready to go beyond the book and actually work with our team to put these strategies into action.

Let's talk about what it means to be part of the *Tax Free Millionaire* Revolution.

What Is the *Tax Free Millionaire* System?

The *Tax Free Millionaire* System is a proprietary program created by our firm—Sarah Jones, CPA. It's designed to create a complete shift in how you think about money, taxes, and wealth both in your business and in your personal life.

This system is only available through our firm. We built it, we live it, and we offer it exclusively to our clients.

How It Works: Your Custom Roadmap

Every new client who comes to Sarah Jones, CPA—whether for general tax planning or the full *Tax Free Millionaire* experience—starts with a custom-built roadmap.

We walk with you through every stage of your business and personal journey, making sure that you're getting the maximum ROI on your tax dollars and financial decisions.

This roadmap becomes your step-by-step plan to:
- Save taxes now
- Build tax-free wealth
- Protect and grow your legacy over time

The Power of the System

Yes, anyone can become a *Tax Free Millionaire*. You don't *have* to be a business owner. But if you *are* one, you've likely been overpaying the IRS for years—and that's where the true power of this system comes in.

We restructure your business, identify tax-saving opportunities, and redirect those savings into tax-free wealth-building accounts—for you, your spouse, and even your children.

This is not theory. This is real, practical implementation. And best of all?

The Roadmap is Affordable

That's right. The *Tax Free Millionaire* Roadmap we offer has an estimated value of $10,000—and we provide it to all of our clients at an affordable price.

Even if you decide not to work with us, you'll walk away with clarity, strategy, and insight into what's *actually* possible when you stop overpaying the IRS and start putting that money to work for your future.

We're Just Getting Started

This is *version 1.0* of *Tax Free Millionaire*, written in 2025. But this movement isn't stopping here. We're already planning versions 2.0, 3.0, 4.0, and beyond—because tax laws will keep changing, and we'll keep adapting to make sure our clients are always ahead of the curve.

So whatever year you're reading this—2026, 2028, 2032—go to www.taxfreemillionairesystem.com and make sure you're accessing the most up-to-date tools and offers.

Your Next Step

Accept our invitation and join the Tax Free Millionaire System. Sarah Jones, CPA is the only firm offering the Tax Free Millionaire System. We built it. We refined it. We live it. This is your opportunity to join us and start building your custom roadmap to a tax-free lifestyle.

- ❏ **Get your *Tax Free Millionaire* Roadmap** – a personalized review valued at $10,000.
- ❏ **Access our exclusive webinar** – where I walk you through updated strategy illustrations (including Tom and Kathy) and break down the system in more depth. This content is updated annually to reflect changes in tax law and strategy implementation.

Simply scan the QR code below or visit www.taxfreemillionairesystem.com to get started.

Let's Rewrite Your Legacy

This isn't just about taxes—it's about your future. We're here to help you legally save 20–30% a year in taxes, reinvest that savings, and use it to build tax-free wealth for yourself, your spouse, and your children. That's how you create real, lasting, generational change. That's how you become a *Tax Free Millionaire*—and empower your family to do the same.

The tools are in place. The strategy is proven.

And the invitation? It's personal.

Let's make it happen.

I can't wait to connect with you, to hear your story, and to help you start this journey.

— Sarah Jones, CPA

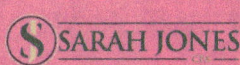

SARAH JONES CPA

The Year-Round Strategic Tax Planning Program is more than just a service, it's a movement. Built around the Tax-Free Millionaire System, this comprehensive, done-for-you financial roadmap is designed to legally minimize tax liability not just once a year, but throughout every year.

Developed by Sarah Jones, CPA, the system reflects her commitment to helping seven- and eight-figure business owners take control of their financial futures with proactive, strategic tax planning. Through elite-level guidance, full implementation support, and IRS-compliant practices, Sarah and her team create customized strategies that protect your legacy and grow your wealth tax-free.

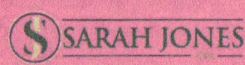

VISION

To revolutionize the way entrepreneurs build, protect and grow wealth by delivering tax strategies that empower financial freedom, peace of mind, and lasting legacy.

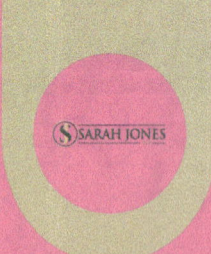

MISSION

At Sarah Jones, CPA, our mission is to deliver year-round, IRS-compliant tax planning that helps high-achieving business owners keep more of what they earn, scale confidently, and create multi-generational wealth strategically, legally, and stress-free.

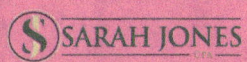
SARAH JONES

OUR CORE VALUES

Integrity

We ensure 100% compliance with tax law. No shortcuts, just smart, and legal strategy.

Proactivity

We don't wait for tax season. We plan ahead to build tax-free financial futures.

Clarity

We provide transparent communication, clear reporting, and real-time guidance.

Empowerment

We educate clients on strategy while handling the heavy lifting behind the scenes.

Legacy

Every plan is designed with long-term wealth, family security, and lasting impact in mind.

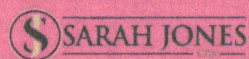

PROGRAM FEATURES

Strategic Onboarding Session
A personalized onboarding session including document collection, team introductions, and a full tech walkthrough to get you set up for success.

Custom 12-Month Roadmap
An annual tax strategy blueprint tailored to your business structure, income streams, and personal goals.

Quarterly Planning Sessions
Four in-depth strategy calls per year to review projections, adjust plans, and seize new opportunities as they arise.

Tax Filing & Year-End Review
Professional tax return filing, paired with a comprehensive savings analysis and future-forward recommendations.

IRS-Compliant Documentation
Full implementation tracking and recordkeeping designed to withstand audits and ensure complete compliance.

Full Strategy Implementation
We do the heavy lifting executing each tax strategy and monitoring performance throughout the year.

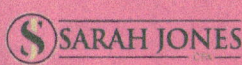

CORE STRATEGIC AREAS

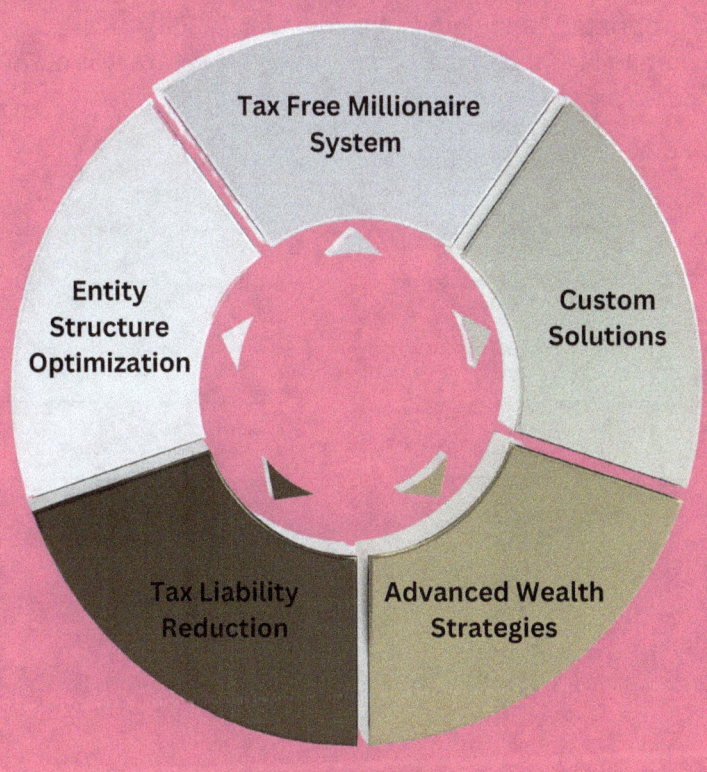

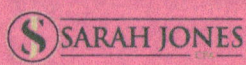SARAH JONES

SOFTWARE & COMPLIANCE TOOLS

Our proprietary technology ensures full visibility, accountability, and audit readiness so your strategy is always executed and IRS-compliant.

1

CUSTOM FINANCIAL DASHBOARD

Personalized dashboard with real-time projections, updated forecasts, and strategic insights tailored to your roadmap.

3

IMPLEMENTATION TRACKER

Live progress tracking to monitor the execution of each tax-saving strategy throughout the year.

2

COMPLIANCE & AUDIT PREP

Built-in systems ensure your strategy meets IRS standards, with documentation designed to withstand audit scrutiny.

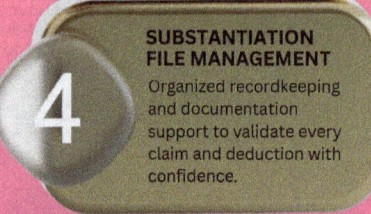

4

SUBSTANTIATION FILE MANAGEMENT

Organized recordkeeping and documentation support to validate every claim and deduction with confidence.

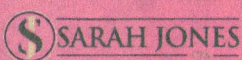
SARAH JONES

BENEFITS

SAVE 20–30% ANNUALLY ON TAXES

Our clients typically save 20% to 30% on taxes each year by leveraging proactive strategies that are tailored to their specific financial situations and business structures.

REDUCE TIME BURDEN

We handle all the heavy lifting so you don't have to. From implementation to compliance, our done-for-you model allows you to stay focused on running your business while we optimize your financial roadmap.

BUILD LONG-TERM, TAX-EFFICIENT WEALTH

We don't just reduce your current tax bill we help you build and preserve wealth over time through tax-efficient investment, retirement, and entity strategies.

ELIMINATE SURPRISE TAX BILLS

With quarterly planning sessions and continuous projections, you'll always know where you stand. No more unexpected tax bills at the end of the year.

ENSURE IRS-COMPLIANT STRUCTURES

Every strategy we implement is fully compliant with IRS guidelines. We maintain detailed documentation to ensure audit readiness and peace of mind.

STRATEGICALLY GROW AND PROTECT ASSETS

Our comprehensive planning approach includes asset protection, estate structuring, and legacy planning ensuring your wealth grows strategically and is preserved for future generations.

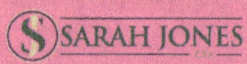
SARAH JONES

SJCPA ROADMAP

01
Discovery & Onboarding Call

We begin with a focused consultation to understand your business structure, goals, and financial landscape. This sets the foundation for a successful partnership.

02
Document Collection & Tech Setup

Our team gathers all essential documents and sets you up with our secure, easy-to-use dashboard to streamline collaboration and track progress in real time.

03
Strategic Launch Session

We introduce you to your advisory team, walk through the tools and systems, and begin building your customized 12-month tax roadmap tailored to your financial goals.

04
Quarterly Strategic Planning Sessions

Every quarter, we revisit your projections and update your strategies to ensure they align with evolving business conditions, and tax law changes.

05
Ongoing Implementation

We handle the heavy lifting executing every tax strategy, maintaining compliance, and proactively optimizing your plan throughout the year.

06
Year-End Filing & Review

Our team files your tax returns and provides a full performance review showing realized savings, tax exposure, and future recommendations.

07
Next-Year Planning Setup

We seamlessly transition into building your next-year roadmap ensuring continuity, refinement, and compounding tax benefits year after year.

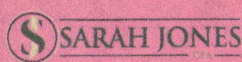

SJCPA BONUSES

Tax-Free Millionaire System

Gain exclusive access to Sarah Jones' signature framework designed to help you build and preserve wealth legally, strategically, and—most importantly—tax-free.

24/7 Access to Your Planning Dashboard

Track your progress, view projections, and monitor strategy implementation in real-time, whenever and wherever it's convenient for you.

New Legislation Strategy Playbooks

Stay ahead of the curve with timely insights and actionable strategies tailored to new tax laws, including major reforms like the Taxonomics Bill.

Full Preparation Cost Included

No surprise fees. Your annual tax return preparation is fully covered within the program, giving you both strategic and compliance benefits in one solution.

Dedicated Support Team

Work with a seasoned team of tax experts, strategists, and client success professionals who guide you through every step of the process with clarity and care.

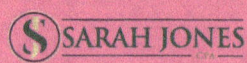

THANK YOU

Partner with SJCPA where innovation meets execution, and your vision becomes reality

📞 +1 936-228-2231

✉ help@sarahjonescpa.com

🌐 sarahjonescpa.com

📍 1336 League Line Rd Suite 300,
Conroe, TX 77304, United States

ENDNOTES

1. James Truslow Adams, The Epic of America (Boston: Little, Brown, 1931), 404.
2. Scott Greenberg, "Federal Tax Laws and Regulations Are Now Over 10 Million Words Long," Tax Foundation (blog), October 8, 2015, accessed July 13, 2025, https://taxfoundation.org/blog/federal-tax-laws-and-regulations-are-now-over-10-million-words-long/.
3. I Timothy 6:10

About the Authors

Sarah and Phil Jones are a powerhouse duo combining financial expertise with practical life and leadership insight.

Sarah Jones is a Certified Public Accountant in the state of Texas and an Enrolled Agent licensed by the IRS in all 50 states. She holds an MBA in Finance, an MS in Accountancy, and an MS in Finance, along with a Certificate in Financial Management from Cornell University. Sarah is also a Certified CFO, Certified Tax Planner, and Certified Exit Planning Advisor. She's the author of Fire My CPA and is passionate about tax strategy—helping clients build their dreams, protect their assets, and grow their legacy.

Phil D. Jones Jr. brings experience in financial planning, ministry, and coaching, with a passion for helping people in everyday ways. He holds a BBA in Finance from Sam Houston State University and a Master of Divinity from Liberty University. With years of experience in both ministry and financial services, Phil brings a grounded, insightful perspective on purpose, leadership, and legacy.

Long-time residents of Willis, Texas, Phil and Sarah have been married since 2011. They share life with their four children and two spoiled French bulldogs. When not serving clients or leading others, they enjoy traveling, working out, and spending time with family.